Other McGraw-Hill Books of Interest

AUTHOR	TITLE	ISBN
Emery	*How to Be a Successful Systems Manager in a PC Environment*	0-07-019639-7 (hc) 0-07-019640-0 (pbk)
Lyon and Gluckson	*MIS Manager's Appraisal Guide: Practical Guidelines and Forms for Evaluating Your MIS Staff*	0-07-039272-2
Ranade and Nash	*The Best of* BYTE	0-07-051344-9
Simon	*The Computer Professional's Survival Guide*	0-07-057574-6
Simon	*How to Be a Successful Computer Consultant, 3/e*	0-07-057617-3 (hc) 0-07-057618-1 (pbk)
Simon and Simon	*The Computer Professional's Guide to Effective Communications*	0-07-057596-7 (hc) 0-07-057597-5 (pbk)
Vassiliou and Orenstein	*The Computer Professional's Quick Reference*	0-07-067211-3 (hc) 0-07-067212-1 (pbk)

Downsized But Not Out

How to Get Your
Next Computer Job

Alan Simon

McGraw-Hill, Inc.

New York   San Francisco   Washington, D.C.   Auckland   Bogotá
Caracas   Lisbon   London   Madrid   Mexico City   Milan
Montreal   New Delhi   San Juan   Singapore
Sydney   Tokyo   Toronto

Library of Congress Cataloging-in-Publication Data

Simon, Alan R.
  Downsized but not out : how to get your next computer job / Alan
R. Simon.
      p.   cm.
  Includes index.
  ISBN 0-07-057614-9—ISBN 0-07-057615-7 (pbk.)
  1. Microcomputers—Vocational guidance.   2. Computer industry—
Employment.   I. Title.
QA76.25.S56   1994
004.16′023—dc20   94-23420
                                                                CIP

1 2 3 4 5 6 7 8 9 0   DOC/DOC   9 0 9 8 7 6 5 4

1 2 3 4 5 6 7 8 9 0   DOC/DOC   9 0 9 8 7 6 5 4

ISBN 0-07-057614-9 (hc)

ISBN 0-07-057615-7 (pbk)

*The sponsoring editor for this book was Marjorie Spencer, the editing
supervisor was Stephen M. Smith, and the production supervisor was
Suzanne W. Babeuf. It was set in Century Schoolbook by McGraw-Hill's
Professional Book Group composition unit.*

Printed and bound by R. R. Donnelley & Sons Company.

This book is printed on recycled, acid-free paper containing
a minimum of 50 percent recycled, de-inked fiber.

Contents

Preface   ix

Part 1   Giving New Life to a Computer Career   1

Chapter 1. And That's the Way It Is   3

1.1 Introduction   3
1.2 Today's Computer Industry and Employment Issues   4
1.3 Skill Set Issues   7
1.4 Chapter Summary   15

Chapter 2. Where Do I Go from Here?   17

2.1 Introduction   17
2.2 Where Am I, and How Did I Get Here?   18
2.3 Self-Assessment   18
2.4 Putting It All Together   28
2.5 Chapter Summary   29

Chapter 3. Interviewing, Résumés, and Other Matters   31

3.1 Introduction   31
3.2 Résumés   31
3.3 So Where Are the Jobs, Anyway?   41
3.4 Interviewing   46
3.5 Corporate Loyalty   50
3.6 It's a Small World, After All...   51
3.7 Chapter Summary   52

Chapter 4. Retraining Yourself for a New Marketplace   55

4.1 Introduction   55

4.2 How I Did It   56
4.3 It Don't Come Easy, You Know It Don't Come Easy   57
4.4 Buy a Computer...Maybe Two!   57
4.5 Formal Training   63
4.6 Staying Current   63
4.7 Chapter Summary   65

Chapter 5. What's Hot Today...and What Will Be Hot Tomorrow   67

5.1   Introduction   67
5.2   New Hardware   67
5.3   New Systems Software   69
5.4   Mobile Computing   69
5.5   Systems Integration   70
5.6   Systems Migration and Transition   71
5.7   Groupware   71
5.8   Workflow   72
5.9   Client/Server Computing   72
5.10 Rapid Prototyping   73
5.11 GUI Development   73
5.12 Chapter Summary   74

Chapter 6. Interim Consulting   75

6.1 Introduction   75
6.2 Defining Your Consulting Goals   75
6.3 Starting a Consulting Practice   78
6.4 Conflicts of Interest and Relationships with Your Former Company   87
6.5 Business Plan   87
6.6 Interviewing for Consulting Positions   88
6.7 Chapter Summary   88

Chapter 7. Lifestyle Adjustment   91

7.1 Introduction   91
7.2 Relocation   91
7.3 Personal Finances   92
7.4 Your Mind-Set   93
7.5 Chapter Summary   94

Part 2   Interviewing   95

Chapter 8. General Interview Questions   99

Chapter 9. Software and Systems Development in the Desktop
Environment   117

Chapter 10. Hardware   131

Chapter 11. Systems Software   147

Chapter 12. Applications Software   159

Chapter 13. Questions That *You* Should Ask   173

Chapter 14. Interviewing for Consultants Only   187

Index   197

Preface

As strange as it might seem for an author to say about his own work, this is an odd book. Actually, it might be more precise to state that this book came about in an odd way. In late 1992, I was discussing plans for doing a third edition of my "flagship" career-oriented book at McGraw-Hill, *How to Be a Successful Computer Consul-tant*. During the course of these discussions, my editor asked me if I would be interested in doing a book about interviewing for jobs in the PC marketplace, primarily oriented toward computer professionals from mainframe and minicomputer arenas who now were being driven, because of market forces, to seek employment in PC-oriented positions. She suggested that the book's format be of a question-and-answer nature, as if simulating an interview.

By coincidence, I had been preparing a proposal for McGraw-Hill for a book about rejuvenating one's career following the sort of career disruption that had become so rampant since the late 1980s, when the great "rightsizing" boom began in corporate America. I had explored titles such as *Giving New Life to a Computer Career* and had planned to include material that expanded on that in my 1991 McGraw-Hill work, *The Computer Professional's Survival Guide*. That book was, and is, more of a general "how to plan for a successful career in the computer field" work, and even though a great deal of material about surviving and thriving in the turbulent times of the early 1990s was included, the emphasis on career *rejuvenation* had not been present (perhaps because as bad as things were beginning to get with respect to career prospects in the 1990–1991 time frame when I was writing that book, things have gotten a whole lot worse since then).

So, I combined the rejuvenation and interviewing ideas to produce a book that contains material about how to retrain and reeducate yourself for the computer marketplace as it stands today, and a representative group of PC-oriented (or, more precisely, desktop-oriented) technical questions.

As we'll discuss in more detail in Chap. 1, long-time computer professionals who find themselves forced to switch from mainframe- or minicomputer-intensive situations to those oriented around PCs and workstations not only face a tremendous amount of difficulty in learning new programming languages (say, C) and new operating systems (for example, UNIX or Windows NT), but are often astonished to find the following: In the mainframe and minicomputer worlds, computer professionals tend to focus on one or two functional areas, such as applications programming or communications-oriented work. Typically, an IBM mainframe MVS COBOL applications programmer will have little to do with, say, LU6.2 protocol work or operations or local area network (LAN) cabling. In such an environment, compartmentalization of personnel resources has been the norm, and entire careers have been built on single niche areas such as complex job control language (JCL) runstream generation and maintenance. *In the desktop arena, this is not true, and those who will succeed often must possess a multitude of skills.* A PC C programmer often must function as

- An applications programmer

- A systems programmer (configuring, say, MS-DOS and Microsoft Windows parameters subject to application and system needs)

- A network specialist, connecting PC clients and servers over, say, a Novell network (with responsibility for such connections in both the hardware and software arenas)

- A systems administrator for both client systems and network servers, configuring user profiles and security constraints in the network server

- A capacity planner, determining what types of processors, what operating system or operating environment, and how much disk space are needed for systems he or she is developing

- A purchasing agent, negotiating with local resellers or mail-order companies for the best prices for his or her company or clients

- A documentation specialist

- A functional analyst

And so on. The point is this: *The career niches of yesteryear, if not totally gone, are on their way out.* A broad base of skills in the many areas we'll explore in this book is an absolute necessity for career flexibility, growth, and survival.

How to Use This Book

The preceding paragraphs should have given you a pretty good idea about the purpose of this book, as well as where the format came from. In general, this book is divided into two parts: ,

Part 1, "Giving New Life to a Computer Career." The material in this part is specifically oriented toward career rejuvenation skills—self-assessment, taking charge of your own career, what technologies are hot today and will be hot tomorrow, etc.—that it is essential you understand. Even if you are, say, a mainframe FORTRAN programmer with a relatively stable company that so far has resisted the downsizing trend (in terms of both technology and personnel—that is to say, it has not moved toward either client/server computing or layoffs), the odds are great that at some point in the next few years, you will be directly or indirectly affected by such a technology shift and the accompanying career disruption. It may not happen at all; you could, perhaps, make it all the way to retirement in the same niche position without being forced to retrain yourself into PCs, Xbase programming, graphical user interfaces (GUIs), and so on. However, I would strongly recommend at least preparing for such a shift to occur.

Part 2, "Interviewing." The chapters in this part are organized by technology (hardware, operating systems and environments, database management, etc.) and are of the sample interview question/typical response type. The questions are *representative*, meaning that when you walk into an interview for, say, a PC database programming position, there is no guarantee that you will be asked all (or even any) of them. These questions are intended to give you some idea of the types of questions you will be asked, and the accompanying material will steer you in the right direction depending on the type of job you're seeking, how technology has changed, and so on.

Acknowledgments

I would like to thank Jeanne Glasser, former computer book editor at McGraw-Hill, for approaching me with this project and helping me steer it into a form which I hope will be valuable to the readers. I would also like to thank Stephen Smith for overseeing the production of this book, and Marjorie Spencer for her guidance during the latter stages of the project.

Alan Simon

Downsized
But Not Out

Giving New Life to a Computer Career

1

And That's the Way It Is

1.1 Introduction

Interviewing stinks. Come on, admit it...it's just you and me talking here, right? No happy facade about how much you're "looking forward to this new opportunity and to making a change that is consistent with where I have envisioned my career heading for the past few years, and whatever-whatever-ya-da-ya-da...." You're looking forward to meeting with a battery of people who will ask you idiotic questions like "Where do you see yourself in five years?" and "What are your strengths and weaknesses?" right? Sure you are....

The plain truth is that many of you reading this book are in remarkably similar circumstances, whether you live in Los Angeles, New York, or Denver, or whether your computer career has been with a software or hardware vendor, an insurance company, a government agency, a manufacturing firm, or whatever else. That is,

> The computer industry, and employment opportunities within that industry or any other industry in which computer technology is widely used, have changed forever.

Even in the "good times"—say, the early and mid-1980s, when computer professionals were kings and queens in American industry—interviewing for a new position was often a distasteful and humbling experience. In *How to Be a Successful Computer Consultant,* I related an experience that I had when I was leaving the Air Force and interviewing for a consulting position at one of the then–Big 8 accounting firms. At the interviewer's request, I had brought along a copy of the first edition of that same book that I had written about computer consulting. During the interview, the interviewer—the branch computer consulting manager—asked to see the book, which I produced for him. I was stunned when, after paging through it for a moment or two, he looked suspiciously at me and asked, "Did you do this yourself?" Not quite sure where he was headed with this line of questioning, I replied in the affirmative that yes, indeed, this was entirely my work, and I launched into the canned speech I always used when asked how I had happened to come up with the idea of writing this book and how I had gone about getting the work published. After a few more "hmmms" and head nods and a few more thumbings through the book, the interviewer *once again* asked me if this really-and-truly-swear-in-court-do-you-know-the-penalties-for-perjury was my own work. Totally confused—and somewhat disgusted—at this point, I clarified that I had (sob!) had a typist do the word processing work for 7 of the 16 chapters, but the words, with the assistance of the friendly staff of copy editors at McGraw-Hill, were *mine and mine alone!* At this point, the subject was changed for another 5 minutes or so until he abruptly rose, announced that he didn't want to be late for his tee time (golf, for those of you who might not recognize the phrase), and departed.

P.S.: I wasn't extended an offer there. Big surprise, huh?

I don't want to ramble on, because you didn't buy this book to read anecdotes about my past interviewing experiences, but I wanted to let you know that however horrific the interview you endured last week, or whatever the ones facing you next week or next month or whenever may bring, they are certainly not isolated incidents nor any reflection on you or your abilities. The plain truth, as I so bluntly stated at the outset of this chapter, is that the interviewing process simply stinks.

1.2   Today's Computer Industry and Employment Issues

And this provides us with an excellent transition to the subject matter of this book. As difficult a process as interviewing is in general, the turmoil in the computer industry with respect to employment and career opportunities has significantly complicated the interviewing function for many of you—indeed, for many of those who would claim the title of computer professionals. Later in this chapter, we'll discuss in detail the forces that are likely to be buffeting your career at this moment. For now, we can assert the following:

The computer industry of today (the mid-1990s) is different not only from the computer industry that existed through the late 1970s, when mainframes ruled the world, but also from that of even a few years ago, the mid- and late 1980s. There are many reasons for this disparity, including

- Changes in hardware technology, from processors to memory to storage media. For example, the PC on which I'm writing this manuscript has 16 megabytes of memory. In late 1987, I was asked during an interview: if I were to configure a Digital Equipment VAX minicomputer or equivalent UNIX midrange system for standard applications processing, how much memory would I put on that system? My answer was 16 megabytes, the same amount of RAM I have sitting in a small box on my desk.

- Changes in software technology, partially driven by the hardware-oriented changes. That 16 megabytes—plus the i486 DX 33-MHz microprocessor—goes a long way toward running integrated software with extremely large documents on a desktop, and has spawned wondrous new applications, graphical user interface (GUI) environments, and the like.

- Dramatic improvements in communications and networking technology, resulting in local area network (LAN), wide area network (WAN), and metropolitan area network (MAN) throughputs and capabilities far superior to those of the recent past.

As a result of these technological advances, many—*not all,* mind you, but many—organizations began to technologically downsize in the late 1980s, and the trend accelerated dramatically through the mid-1990s. We need to emphasize the "not all" qualifier above because this book and its contents should not be viewed in the light of the simplistic "the mainframe is dead, long live PCs that do everything for everyone" proposition, and its corollary that each and every mainframe COBOL, FORTRAN, and PL/I programmer; every VAX/VMS systems administrator; and every SNA network architect is immediately out of a job unless he or she learns to convincingly sing the praises of his or her desktop computing capabilities. The mainframe will live, not only in coexistence with desktop systems in many (perhaps most) large organizations, but in some companies retaining its position as the only solution for the data center.

Despite the qualifications in the above paragraph, the outlook for long, illustrious, and rewarding career paths centered exclusively around mainframe and minicomputer hardware and software technology has entered a dramatic downward spiral in the past 3 to 5 years. Even in large multinational corporations that nay-say the capabilities of desktop LAN-based computing and that have a large stockpile of mainframe-based information systems assets (applications, data), individual departments and their leaders no longer can afford the long application development backlogs that are typical in centralized, mainframe-based environments. The minicomputer trend that took off in the 1970s and flew high in the 1980s primarily because of Digital Equipment Corporation's VAX/VMS systems was the first indication of this departmental-level impatience, and the technological advances in desktop systems discussed above have only fueled this impatience. Rather than wait patiently for months or years for the data center folks to provide applications which are often out of date when finally delivered, they have empowered themselves by building departmental-class applications around desktop systems, very often in LANs featuring servers and PC client systems.

Accompanying this technology paradigm shift have been the well-publicized *personnel*-oriented downsizings in corporate America (and, for that matter, around the world) that also began in the late 1980s and also have dramatically accelerated. (To be fair, you could point to the deep recession in the 1980–1982 time frame and the corporate cutbacks that accompanied that downturn as the start of deep *Fortune* 500–class personnel cuts, but these cuts were offset by the tremendous economic growth in the mid-1980s. Regardless of the actual starting point for large corporate-level downsizings, it is unarguable that the trend has hit high gear, and today we hear terms like "the jobless economic recovery," referring to the United States' coming out of recession with far weaker job growth than had followed recessions of the past.)

Just so you don't think the above is simply your Economics 101 class revisiting you in a nightmare, there is a great deal of pertinence to personnel cuts and the other items discussed above. Consider the following:

- Large companies are either shedding thousands or even tens of thousands of workers, or at best just aren't hiring nearly as much as they once did.

- These cuts often hit in large numbers in "support functions," such as public relations, purchasing, *and data processing.*

- These data processing cuts are often aimed at the data center staff, meaning that (1) far fewer positions in other companies are available for displaced computer professionals as well as those just entering the job market (e.g., new graduates), and (2) the dramatically downsized data center staff has an ever-increasing backlog of applications and systems to be developed, even if mainframe and minicomputer systems are not being replaced by smaller-scale computing environments.

- Because of the above, department managers are more likely than ever to turn to small-scale departmental-class information systems solutions that can be quickly developed with relative ease, more often than not built around desktop computing environments. Therefore, the relatively small numbers of positions which will see any kind of growth in employment numbers will increasingly be those most critical to those departmental end users—that is, those oriented toward PC and other desktop technologies.

Putting all this together, we see that there will be limited computer professional employment growth in general and extremely limited employment growth in traditional mainframe and minicomputer positions in particular, and that information systems solutions demands among the user base will be dramatically shifted toward PC and desktop technologies.

1.3   Skill Set Issues

OK, you may be thinking, so the platform base of a great deal of the present and future computer systems development in corporate America (and the accompanying employment opportunities) is shifting toward desktop solutions. No problem. If I can do BAL assembler programming or if I can write CICS transaction processing monitor routines on big, powerful mainframe systems, then surely I can do...well, whatever on some toy PCs. Hey, you said that your PC has 16 megabytes of RAM just like the typical VAX minicomputer once did, so obviously I can take mainframe-class or minicomputer-class applications development skills and make the transition into the PC arena, right?

In one sense, that has some truth to it, given, for example, that COBOL programs can be developed on PC platforms using a system such as Microfocus COBOL, and that many of the database management systems from the mainframe and minicomputer worlds (primarily the relational ones, though), such as Oracle, Informix, and now even IBM's DB2, have PC and desktop equivalents that function nearly identically to their larger system versions. However, this direct mapping is only a small part of the equation with respect to downsizing your skill set along with your computing environments. Let's explore some of the issues with respect to this area.

1.3.1   Different implementation paradigms

Let's assume for a moment that you are a traditional mainframe COBOL programmer charged with developing an application in a desktop-oriented environment, and that you have the entire universe of developmental languages, tools, run-time utilities, and the like at your disposal. Following the line of thinking above, you could conceivably develop an application on an ordinary desktop PC that exhibits all the characteristics of one that would be found in a mainframe environment:

- COBOL source code
- A centralized application architecture, with "terminals"—perhaps user PCs doing terminal emulation—running portions of the application in parallel with one another, using multitasking capabilities of the PC server system
- A character-based terminal interface like that which would be found on 3270-family terminals
- A centralized database on your server system, with all user accesses to that database controlled via the application

And so on. There is one problem, though: Most users *do not want* this type of application and system architecture in a desktop environment! They want the wondrous capabilities which PC users have come to know and love: graphical user interfaces, local user-based control over data assets (e.g., spreadsheet data, personal filing systems, etc.), rapidly developed systems using fourth-generation languages (4GLs) or CASE-based code generators, and similar features. Further, they want easily maintained code, perhaps code that could even be maintained by the users if the 4GL or CASE-based implementation were easy to understand. They even want things which they probably don't fully understand, except that they've heard and read a lot about these wondrous technologies and know that they represent goodness—concepts such as object orientation and client/server computing. *The user community does not want business as usual, only on a smaller scale; it wants "change."* (Sounds a lot like a certain recent presidential election, right?)

1.3.2   Different development paradigms

In part because of the items discussed above, traditional "waterfall" development methodologies (see Fig. 1.1) common to large mainframe and minicomputer environments (such as the U.S. Department of Defense's 2167A standard), where a complete set of requirements is

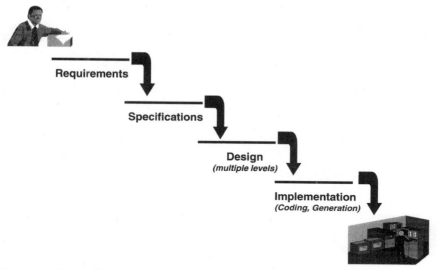

Figure 1.1 The traditional systems development methodology.

gathered; specifications are developed; a complete set of conceptual, logical, and implementation-specific designs is created; coding and/or systems integration takes place; and years later a probably-out-of-date system is achieved—well, to be blunt, the customers aren't buying this any more.

What are highly desired by much of today's user community is proof-of-concept, try-before-buy, prototyping-oriented development paradigms. I'm a COBOL programmer from way back, and I cringe every time I hear a computer science type badmouth COBOL as voluminous, lacking in "neat" features, out of date, and pretty much the cause of most of the world's evils. What I will concede, though, is that one of the biggest knocks against COBOL is that it takes too long to produce applications (or portions thereof), and that entire systems developed in COBOL are often out of date when delivered primarily because of the prolonged coding and implementation time frame.

However, *the same is true for every other third-generation language (3GL) as well.* C, Pascal, Ada—*all* 3GLs suffer from the same slow development style. As a result, a great deal of PC and desktop development has been in the form of 4GLs, database platforms, CASE-based code generators, and the like instead of 3GLs, even though C, COBOL, and most other languages are available.

This isn't to state that almost no 3GL usage on PC platforms has existed or will exist; C and Pascal are especially popular for PC platforms, and their respective development life cycles have been speeded by tools and environments such as Borland's TurboPascal and TurboC. However, 4GLs, database platforms, and other rapid development tools have gained favor among users and developers who strive for quick turnaround time.

Because of the growth of rapid development tools, methodologies have shifted somewhat to accommodate the quick turnaround that is now increasingly possible. Instead of gathering a monolithic set of requirements, as would be done in a waterfall-type methodology, a typical paradigm might be more like the following:

1. Determine the business needs and requirements for one or two functional areas.

2. Develop a rapid prototype, using screen generators, 4GLs, or the tool(s) of your choice.

3. See what you come up with, and run it by your user community. If they like it, build on it by adding more functionality or moving on to other business areas. If they don't, find out why, throw the system away, and start over. It probably only took you a few days, a few weeks, or perhaps a month or so to develop it anyway!

Such environments tend to be spiral in nature in that instead of

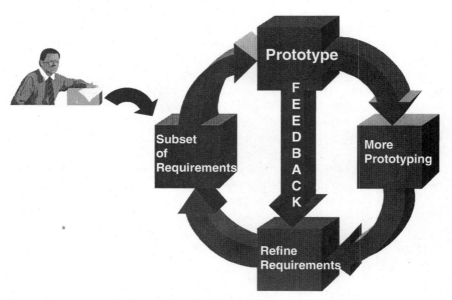

Figure 1.2   An example of a spiral methodology suited to rapid development.

one stage of the development flowing into the next as over a waterfall, any stage—such as requirements collection or coding and development—is likely to be visited several times (perhaps more) as the system rapidly grows from a simple concept, perhaps a few prototype screens, to an entire system (see Fig. 1.2).

You have to recognize this and know how to do this if you are to successfully move your skill set and career path from the mainframe or minicomputer world to the desktop. If you insist on proceeding with traditional, 1970s-era development methodologies, your chances for success in the desktop information systems arena will be reduced, regardless of whether you have learned how to, for example, program client/server, GUI-based applications in C or not. Just as coding does not stand alone in the mainframe arena—it must be accompanied by the other life-cycle stages, such as requirements analysis and design—coding skills applicable to the desktop must also be accompanied by an understanding of *how* software is developed in such an environment.

1.3.3 Development platforms

In the previous section, we mentioned how in many cases 3GL development in languages such as COBOL and FORTRAN is giving way to newer development tools, such as 4GLs and database platforms. Consider the following:

If you are a COBOL programmer for database applications, chances are that your programs will make SQL or DL/I calls to an underlying database management system, one which is a totally separate software environment. In the PC arena, however, this most often is not the case. Xbase programs—those based on the dBASE programming language that originated with Ashton-Tate's family of dBASE products and was adapted by other products such as Clipper and FoxPro (see Chaps. 11 and 12)—are commonly developed in a self-contained environment (although, as we'll discuss in Chap. 12, this is slowly shifting because of client/server computing pressures). Figure 1.3 compares the structure of a traditional mainframe database program with that of one written in an Xbase language. Note that in the PC Xbase environment of today, the language, data management environment, tools, utilities, and run-time environment are closely integrated with one another, unlike in the more traditional alternative.

No, I would not want to develop communications drivers in Xbase; I'd rather use C or Ada or even assembly language. Yes, in the purist's sense, an Xbase system such as dBASE IV or FoxPro is not a "real" relational database management system as defined in E. F.

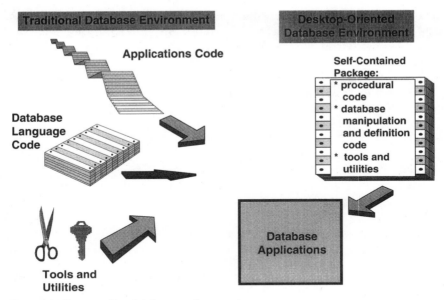

Figure 1.3 Comparative database environments.

Codd's seminal paper from 1970 (although most database experts would argue that SQL-based relational systems aren't truly relational, either). However, for the most part, *your user community doesn't care in the least*; they want to see applications, and they want to see them *quickly*. Comprehensive platforms such as FoxPro are often among the best choices for such rapid development, and skills in this area can greatly aid your transition into the desktop arena.

1.3.4 Off-the-shelf integration

Integration of off-the-shelf software is hardly unique to the desktop marketplace; third-party commercial application offerings have been present in the mainframe and midrange arenas for years, and many computer professionals in the large-system realm have built careers around development with and usage of such packages. With the advent of the PC and the growth of all types of desktop systems throughout the 1980s and into the 1990s, the availability of commercial applications and subsystems has increased dramatically, and many computer professionals specializing in desktop environments often find themselves serving more as system integrators than as traditional application developers. A software package here, another one there, some "interface glue" to make the two talk to one another, and presto: instant system!

As a result of the growth of such integration paradigms, it is no longer sufficient for computer professionals to be programming-literate (or even software development–literate, in a broader sense) at the expense of integration skills. "Systems development" in the desktop domain often entails a great deal of such integration, and the ability to do it is crucial to long-term career success.

1.3.5 A broader skills base

Finally, as we discussed briefly in the Preface, in the desktop arena, unlike in the more traditional mainframe and minicomputer realms, computer professionals often have to wear *many* hats. It is rare that you can consider yourself "simply an applications programmer," safely distancing yourself from the many other disciplines that make up computer systems development (and, for that matter, maintenance).

This point was driven home to me very early in my computer career in general, and my consulting career in particular. During the four years I was an Air Force computer systems officer, I also ran a consulting business specializing in small business applications. In my Air Force life, I programmed on Unisys (then Sperry-Univac) 1100 mainframe systems in a 3GL called JOVIAL (with some assembly language usage as well, since I was doing systems and communications programming). Most of my colleagues did little other than write applications programs and an occasional job control runstream; because of the communications programming I was doing, I was also peripherally involved with some hardware issues, such as specifying what type of communications boards would be needed when we added a new interface circuit, what the synchronization character setting would be for the board strappings, and other matters like that.

Even this minor hardware interaction in my Air Force position paled against the degree of involvement on the PC side in my consulting life, though. For most of my clients, I would

- Perform functional analysis, procedural and database design, and trade-off studies for their proposed systems.

- Make recommendations as to the development platforms I would utilize (typically dBASE II, III, or III+).

- Evaluate and make recommendations about commercial off-the-shelf PC software solutions, such as integrated accounting packages, word processors, and spreadsheets.

- Analyze proposed modem-based dial-up interfaces to remote services as part of their overall systems functionality.

- Make recommendations about the type of hardware platform(s), including processor type (in the early days, a typical question was, "Is it worth going with an IBM PC-AT, or should I stick with a basic PC?"), hard disk capacity, main memory ("Do I really need to put a megabyte of memory on this system?"), and peripheral devices such as tape backups and scanners.

- Do screen design in accordance with user interface principles, user preferences, and other factors.

- Analyze network requirements and make LAN recommendations with regard to server types, whether the server should be dedicated or should be permitted to function as a user workstation as well, what LAN software would be needed, etc.

- Perform system support functions, such as configuration management and testing.

- Write data and program backup scripts.

- Provide both telephone and on-site operational assistance and problem resolution, not only in my applications (when I would make that rare mistake!), but also for system-related problems such as hard disk crashes, degraded network performance, network-based printer timeouts, etc.

This list doesn't even include the consulting- and business-oriented functions I found myself doing, such as bids and proposals, business development, billing and management, subcontractor management and control, staying up to date with the endless stream of new hardware and software products, and similar tasks. The point should be obvious, though, and if you only remember one thing from this chapter, it should be this:

> As you move your career into the desktop arena, whether oriented toward traditional personal computers or high-end workstations, your skills base must be significantly broader than it probably was in your previous mainframe- or minicomputer-oriented life. This breadth is essential if you are to succeed, because your competitors—those people coming into the PC job market without the legacy of years in more traditional computing environments—already have those skills.

As I've stated several times earlier in this chapter, the skills base that you bring to your new career prospects is not simply a one-for-one transition from your previous career base. You may be one of the lucky folks who not only was a COBOL or FORTRAN programmer but also got a chance to do LU6.2 communications, perhaps work with SNA or DECNet capabilities in depth, and be responsible for configuration management as an "additional duty." It is more likely, though, that your previous career path was narrower in scope, perhaps you focused exclusively on 3270 terminal hardware interfaces and cabling, and did little software-based network configuration and management and no application programming at all. Or perhaps you focused exclusively on JCL and operations-related items (perhaps managing large-scale system backup and recovery), but didn't need to know much about other aspects of systems control and programming (device identifiers, boot tape configurations, etc.).

The point is, to emphasize it again, that in the desktop-oriented environment in which you will probably find yourself, you must strive to prove yourself to be a jack-of-all-trades and additionally, unlike the phrase, a master of most or all of them.

1.4 Chapter Summary

In this chapter, we've focused primarily on setting the stage for our discussion in the subsequent chapters. It's important to note that our intention has not been to provide a doom-and-gloom outlook for the career of each and every person working in the mainframe and mini-computer worlds, including those who have not yet been affected by what has happened to so many others. The point is, though, that you should recognize potential storm clouds on the horizon and—as is my theme in most of my career-oriented books—take charge of your own career and *empower yourself.*

You absolutely have to recognize the trends today and extrapolate how they may affect your career:

1. Computer platforms are changing, with the "toys" so many data center professionals sneered at for so many years—PCs— irrefutably considered capable of supporting many different classes of applications.

2. Computer users' patience with the long backlogs for application development in the mainframe and minicomputer arenas is wearing thin; they are under the same career pressures most of us are ("Produce *now* or don't let the door hit you as you're leaving! Do I make myself clear, Snerdly?"), and they want their computer applications and systems faster than ever before at less cost than ever before. PCs and desktop systems are the medium through which these demands are most commonly being met.

3. The trend in business in general, and now in many governmental entities, is toward leaner staffs. The folks that pay the salaries

don't want a staff full of operators, full-time testers, point-product application developers ("I only do COBOL, and only for insurance billing applications"), and costly hardware maintenance contracts.

In many cases, the two types of downsizing—people and technology—have a chicken-and-egg relationship, in that fewer people (read: lower costs) is the edict from the board of directors ("Cut 10,000 people over the next 2 years; I don't care where you do it, and don't affect operations, either!"), and one of the few ways this may be achieved is by making the transition to lower-cost technology (read: PCs and LANs). Conversely, moving to more "modern" desktop technology requires computer professionals with a different skill set from that required in more traditional environments, and guess what? "If we downsize in the technology realm, we can do so also in the people arena," the thoughts go.

Therefore, whether technology or cost savings is the driver, the trend is clear, both for corporate America (indeed, worldwide business) and for your careers. Be prepared!

2

Where Do I Go from Here?

2.1 Introduction

In the previous chapter, we discussed the environmental constraints under which you are probably making your job search. Note that except for a few instances, we have yet to discuss the main topic of this book, *interviewing,* and certainly not in much detail. I would ask that you bear with me for one more chapter before we discuss some basics of interviewing—and, more specifically, interviewing for PC-oriented positions.

The reason is that before you walk into an interviewer's office, before you subject yourself to a phone screen from an HR (human resources, or personnel) type, before you even visit a recruiter (head-hunter) or answer an ad you see in the paper, it is *essential* that you have some idea of where you are headed as you embark on or continue with a job search.

This doesn't mean that you should spend an extraordinary amount of time on this process; for many of you, time may be of the essence with respect to finding a new position quickly. Financial pressures, family concerns, and the like may drive you to either grab the first position offered or short-circuit the retraining process discussed in this book.

Even if your particular situation dictates such hurried action, you should still attempt to pursue the self-assessment and planning activities advocated here. As you are no doubt aware, all jobs are *not* created equal, and even if you successfully make the transition into the desktop computing market, there is no guarantee that (1) your new company, (2) your new position, or (3) any other job factors are what you need or what is best for you. You may not find the optimum situation the first time around, but at least if you set some level of objectives within the bounds of a consolidated career plan, you can eventually shift your efforts towards areas you want.

2.2   Where Am I, and How Did I Get Here?

Before you can figure out where you and your career are headed, it's important to have a good understanding of just where you really are and how you got to this point. Chances are that you fit into one of the following categories:

1. You have just been laid off (or are about to be), have accepted a voluntary severance package of some type, or have resigned from your current organization (for any one of a number of reasons).

2. You are still employed on a full-time basis, but you are working primarily in what you perceive to be a career dead end, one from which you have not been able to extricate yourself, no matter how hard you've tried. Perhaps you've volunteered for new pilot development programs—ones which utilize newer, more interesting (and more marketable in terms of your skills base) technology— but you have been denied access to these efforts. While it's possible that some of your coworkers have been given these opportunities, it's more likely that the new kids in town, perhaps recent college graduates, are assigned to these high-profile efforts, even though they probably earn significantly less money at present than you and others with your tenure at your firm. You see the handwriting on the wall; you realize that when a critical mass of applications has been developed on desktop platforms, and when the newcomers understand the business functions of the company as well as you "old-timers," there is likely to be a shift toward the desktop computing crowd with respect to career growth, if not outright job security (i.e., if job cuts need to be made, those individuals most familiar with newer technologies are likely to be the ones retained).

2.3   Self-Assessment

Let's assume that (1) your time frame for seeking PC-related employment is something other than within the next week and that (2) you want to ensure that the position you eventually land is one in keeping with your (probably newly revised) career objectives, not just a variable-term job simply to bring in a paycheck.

One of the first things you should do is to conduct a thorough, *honest,* and insightful self-assessment. By self-assessment I mean an investigation of your past successes and shortcomings—and *why* you were successful in some situations but not in others—as well as trying to determine where you want to head from this point in your career...and in your life.

Your assessment should focus on four areas:

1. Your technical skills

2. Your "business" (for lack of a better word; I'll elaborate on this term shortly) acumen

3. Your anticipated career path (stay technical? return to the technical side? try consulting, either short-term or long-term?)

4. Your personal assets and other personal factors

It isn't enough, for example, to inventory your technical skills that are (or aren't) applicable to PC hardware and software technologies; you should have as complete as possible an understanding of where you want to head in order to (1) direct your job searches in the right direction and (2) evaluate the opportunities that come your way.

Let's look at each of these areas in more detail.

2.3.1 Technical skills

In the first chapter we discussed how it is erroneous—and dangerous—to assume that there is a one-for-one mapping of mainframe or minicomputer skills to the desktop arena. That is, it is not only erroneous but dangerous as well, if you are a PL/I applications programmer who deals very little with hardware, operations, systems management, and other facets of information systems, to assume that the same job paradigm will more or less carry over to the PC marketplace. Unless you *clearly* understand this, you will be at a severe disadvantage in all aspects of competing for a PC-oriented position, from consideration based on your résumé to interviews.

It's rather simplistic, though, to consider our discussion in the first chapter of PC professionals performing a much broader range of functions than mainframe or minicomputer staffers without assessing *your own personal aptitudes in these many areas,* knowing where you have weaknesses, and developing a plan to shore up those weaknesses.

Following our example of an applications programmer with little hands-on hardware experience, let's consider the types of hardware-oriented functions a PC computer professional is often called upon to perform:

- Installing boards into expansion slots. While this often is fairly trivial, you do come across many board installations that give the "put tab A into slot B, but not before spring C is attached to hooks D1 and D2 and not after…" instructions found with children's toys a run for their money with respect to lack of clarity. You need to be able to follow instructions; unlike with software, there is little room for "freelancing" (i.e., there is often only *one* correct solution to installing hardware, not numerous solutions with one or two that are better than others).

- Installing new disk drives, or replacing old ones. Like installing expansion boards, disk drive work requires close following of instructions. Whereas the data center staff typically handles this type of function in large-scale environments, the PC professional often must perform tasks like this himself or herself (though, in many cases, organizations have service contracts with local retailers or support agencies that do the more complex hardware maintenance and upgrades).

- Installing local area network hardware, from relatively simple tasks like hooking up a new PC or workstation to an existing network to building an entire network from scratch [server(s) and workstations, and all cabling, connectors, and other components]. PC professionals invariably must deal with LAN environments, since the stand-alone PC is pretty much a rarity in the environments in which you are likely to find yourself.

- Upgrading CPUs or memory; for example, you may be charged with upgrading a department's PCs from various i486 microprocessors to Pentium processors. Likewise, you may be charged with upgrading the RAM on those same systems by adding memory chips.

For these and similar tasks, you should have some experience with and aptitude for working with "things." Many software-oriented professionals (myself included, I must admit) tend to function more in a conceptual, abstract manner, and unless they are mechanically inclined in general, they may be wary about tasks such as installing disk drives into PCs. If you fall into this category, you should consider taking a short course in basic PC-oriented hardware functions and maintenance (see Chap. 4 for more discussion of retraining).

2.3.2 Business acumen

While many of you may have worked in a variety of different industries during your career, and in some cases your experience base might be rather broad (for example, 10 years in the aerospace and defense business and another decade in the insurance industry), many others of you may have only a single base of experience. Perhaps you have spent your entire career working on military computer systems, or, more specifically, you have focused exclusively on embedded systems such as onboard missile guidance systems. Note that "business" acumen doesn't necessarily have to be business-oriented; rather, it refers to experience and expertise within a certain applications area. Onboard missile guidance systems or biogenetics research would qualify as such.

Just as your technology range may be rather narrow given the path your career has taken up to this point (for example, your missile guidance systems may have been written exclusively in assembly language), your functional area knowledge (business acumen) may also lack breadth. This isn't to denigrate your functional expertise, mind you. You may be a world-class expert in embedded software systems for air-to-air missiles, but the market and political forces have put your life's work in jeopardy. As you might guess, certain business areas (such as missile guidance) don't transfer well to the PC marketplace, and résumé screeners, interviewers, and hiring authorities may discount your expertise because it isn't applicable to their businesses.

Let's take the alternative, though, and assume that perhaps you have written health insurance applications for IBM mainframes for the past two decades. Given the radical overhaul of the U.S. healthcare system that is likely to occur through the rest of the decade, and the tremendous amount of information systems support required for that overhaul, you could rightfully assume that your functional knowledge, your business acumen, is directly transferable to the desktop arena.

But, as part of the insightful self-assessment that is advocated here, you *must* ask yourself the following question: If I were offered a job tomorrow working in the same business area as I currently do, except that it would be on more modern technology such as desktop systems, *would I accept?*

To be fair and honest with yourself, you should ask yourself this question without regard to financial and other considerations. That is, if you currently work in a relatively high-paying industry and your current lifestyle is predicated on your current income level, try to factor that out of the equation. Don't ask yourself, "If I could find a PC-oriented position that pays just as much as I currently earn (or most recently earned, if you are out of the workforce), would I accept?" Ask yourself, *"Am I happy doing what I'm doing?"* And, of course, the corollary question should also be asked: "If I'm not happy in such-and-such a business area, where would I be happier?"

As we'll discuss shortly, personal factors such as financial obligations certainly do enter into the self-assessment process, so don't assume that we advocate cavalierly disregarding such real-world concerns. Rather, *before* you embark on your position search, you need to have some idea of the area(s) in which you would like to concentrate. Like it or not, many hiring managers place a premium on functional experience in the applications for which they are responsible. If, following a career doing banking software, you decide that you would be happier, that your work would be more fulfilling, in clinical medical systems, *you had better start preparing now.*

2.3.3 Anticipated career path

In *The Computer Professional's Survival Guide,* I noted that in a general sense, there are two primary paths you may pursue during your information systems career: technical and managerial (Fig. 2.1). Though there have been cutbacks of late among organizations with formal dual-track career paths, that paradigm nonetheless defines the directions you will take in the future, as well as that which you have pursued in the past.

In a traditional context, your "normal" career path would start with being a programmer/analyst or other task-oriented technical staff member, then progress to team leadership and supervisory roles and eventually through the managerial ranks. As your career progressed, your technical involvement would become less and less, and you would be expected to focus your efforts on managerial tasks such as staff planning, budgeting, strategic and tactical planning, and similar functions.

In contrast, technical-track professionals would forgo the tradition-

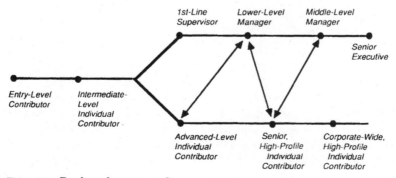

Figure 2.1 Dual-track career paths.

al managerial functions as they progressed, instead pursuing "guru status" in one or more technology areas, typically in a cross-project or cross-program manner. For example, a technical-track database expert would function as an adviser to multiple projects within a company on database and information management matters, as well as providing strategic direction to I.S. managers and planners with respect to database product evaluation and selection and similar tasks.

As was pointed out in *The Computer Professional's Survival Guide,* and as is probably obvious to you given the subject matter of this book, the more traditional managerial track can arguably be considered obsolete. That is, the stereotypical nontechnical manager who relies on his or her staff for nearly every technical matter, the person who may be viewed (fairly or not) as little more than a paper pusher, is an endangered species in these days of cutthroat organizational slashing. Project leaders, program managers, and group managers must have some degree of technical competence in order to survive in the 1990s.

So how does this paradigm apply specifically to the PC and desktop computing environment, and more specifically to the process of locating employment related to such technologies?

Consider what your career path has been to date. Have you risen through the ranks to mid-level or senior management, letting your technical skills erode as your career progressed? If so, your retraining effort may well be a bit more complex than that of a more hands-on technologist, even if the latter's skills are mainframe- or minicomputer-oriented. That is, if you have never used a CASE tool, if the last time you personally developed any type of application was when Gerald Ford was president, if you haven't personally installed a software package on any type of system—from PC to mainframe—since the early days of your career, you have somewhat more catching up to do than the displaced COBOL programmers and systems administrators *who probably are going after the same jobs you are.*

This is not to state that after a career in management, you are expected or will have to significantly drop back to developer status (or a similar level). It is very likely that you will be able to make the transition from a mainframe-oriented or minicomputer-oriented manager to a similar level of responsibility in an organization with a desktop computing focus. However, you will no longer be able to stay as detached from technology as you may have been up to this point, and your success in both finding a position and keeping it may well be determined by your technical expertise as well as your managerial abilities.

Scan through the classifieds of a newspaper such as *The New York Times,* and you will see positions of the following type:

MIS Manager—Manhattan-based company seeks hands-on person to lead small team in implementing LAN-based client/server. Must have hands-on Novell and MS Windows. Hands-on C or C++ desirable. Salary commensurate with experience.

It may be odd to think of a person with the title of MIS manager as needing hands-on Novell NetWare, Microsoft Windows, and C or C++ to be able to function in his or her job, but this is representative of more than a few positions today. Today's MIS manager, especially in PC-oriented environments, is expected to possess some degree of competence with *today's* technologies.

The important thing is to understand *both* the paths you've taken in the past *and* where you'd like to be. Assessing the past might appear to be of little benefit; after all, you've done what you've done, and it's all there on the table, isn't it? The positions you've held, the times you've switched companies and jobs, the promotions you've received—it's all an open book, right?

Not so fast. It's critical to assess *why* you've made the career moves you've made (or, in some cases, *haven't* made, as in jobs you were offered but turned down). Consider the following:

Let's say that you began your career as a VAX FORTRAN programmer, and after a year or so you moved to a full-time testing position, where you rose through the ranks to become the manager of a testing group, the position you hold today.

It's important to *honestly* assess why you switched from being a FORTRAN programmer to being a tester. Was it because the task leader of the testing group was scheduled to leave the organization the following year, and this appeared to be your quickest path to a position with more pay and responsibility?

Or was it because you were having trouble as a FORTRAN programmer; applications development just wasn't coming naturally to you, and even though you liked working with computers, you wanted to find some other type of position that didn't directly involve coding and development?

There is no "right" or "wrong" reason for making that particular career move (as well as others), just the *real* reason. It's important that you honestly grasp the real reason because any job search you are currently pursuing or are about to pursue should be done with all of these factors in mind, in order to permit you to make the most intelligent decisions.

Let's assume that you admit to yourself that you made that particular career switch to testing because you were having troubles in your job—you just weren't doing that well. If so, *why* was that the case?

Perhaps it was because you were doing systems programming, and your academic training had been more oriented toward applications programming. With little background in things like multiprocessing architectures, queues and other data structures, and the other tools of the systems programming trade—and little more than on-the-job training to help you overcome that lack of background—you were more or less lost.

Solution for your current or upcoming job search: You should probably avoid systems programming and focus instead on organizations that are involved more in applications development. This would be true even without the technology paradigm shift away from large systems toward desktop computing.

Or perhaps you were doing applications programming, but the applications were scientific and mathematical in nature, and your academic background and prior training had been more business-oriented, perhaps involving inventory and sales management systems. You had trouble grasping the mathematical modeling concepts and creating the necessary algorithms, let alone coding them.

Solution for your current or upcoming job search: Stay away from applications areas that are similar to those which have given you trouble in the past. Instead, focus on business-oriented applications. As with our previous example, this would be true even if you were pursuing minicomputer-related employment; there is little sense in heading into a development position in an area for which you may not have the aptitude.

On the other side of the career track, let's consider the following. Perhaps you have pursued a technical track, deliberately avoiding any supervisory or managerial responsibility and choosing instead to focus exclusively on computer and communications technology. It could be that you pursued several opportunities on the technical side of your current or former organization's dual-track career path, and that those opportunities allowed you to advance and receive compensation in excess of that which you would have had if you had stayed on the supervisory and managerial side.

However, it could also be that you have avoided any sort of managerial or supervisory responsibility because you don't feel comfortable doing anything other than dealing directly with computer systems development. You didn't want to get involved with systems cost planning or procurement, or with leading others.

As we have noted, positions in the desktop computing realm tend to require a broader base of skills than are needed for larger systems, where there is greater division of labor. If you have chosen to avoid all but a narrow range of responsibilities, this could put you at a disadvantage in both finding and succeeding at a new position.

So what does all this mean with respect to assessing your career path? Simply that unless you are a phenomenal individual with an unending depth and breadth of talents, you have professional strengths and weaknesses like every other one of us, and in many cases, those strengths and weaknesses have directly influenced the career choices you have made in the past. Given the types of positions you are likely to be pursuing in the PC-oriented marketplace, it's critical that you understand those strengths and weaknesses, *how* they have influenced your past decisions, and *whether* or not you need to overcome certain weaknesses in order to facilitate your job search and increase your chances for success once you find a new position. In Chap. 4, we'll discuss the process of retraining yourself for this new age of desktop-oriented technology in more detail.

2.3.4 Personal considerations

Finally, no assessment is complete without an understanding of your personal situation, particularly in the following areas:

1. *Financial situation.*   How do your savings account and emergency funds stash look? Could you afford to be away from a full-time earning position for three or six months, or perhaps a year, while you attempt to acquire new skills that will make you more marketable in today's job market? Does your spouse or "significant other" have a salary that would be sufficient to provide such support? How does your personal balance sheet (assets vs. debts) look?

2. *Career choice.*   In addition to our previous discussion about career paths you have taken and will pursue in the future in the computer industry, you should also ask yourself, am I really happy working with computers for a living? If not, switching to another career may be desirable, perhaps one in which you *use* computers as a support tool (e.g., doing financial analysis on spreadsheets, managing lists using a database, etc.) rather than as the primary focus of your job. Maybe moving away from, say, your mainframe-oriented career to one in which PCs play an important role may provide just the boost you need to regain your enthusiasm as a computer professional, but maybe it won't. If feasible (e.g., subject to financial considerations and other factors), maybe your search should shift focus to some other line of work.

3. *Risk tolerance.*   As we'll discuss in Chap. 6, one of the paths you

might pursue—either on an interim basis or as an entirely new career path—is consulting, in lieu of full-time, career-track employment. In fact, given the technology focus shift that we're discussing, such a switch from your current employment-based career to one oriented toward project-based consulting may be a natural movement. However, you have to have some degree of tolerance for risk and uncertainty. Assessing your degree of risk tolerance is crucial in determining where you want to concentrate your efforts (e.g., trying to find a full-time job or seeking consulting projects).

4. *Environmental and external factors.* While these are not directly "personal considerations"—that is, items over which you have control—you should thoroughly assess environmental factors such as the local economy, the health of the industry in which you have most of your experience, and similar things. If you are committed to remaining in your local area, what does the job market look like? At the time this is being written, the national economy in the United States is showing some signs of strength, but if you're in California, New York, Connecticut, or New Jersey, you are unlikely to see that, as these areas (which outperformed the national economy during most of the 1980s) are still struggling back to financial stability. Finding a position, whether it involves PC technology or not, is likely to be significantly more difficult in certain areas within these states than in, say, Denver, which had its own problems during most of the 1980s. I can personally attest to the effect of regional economic factors on job searches, having lived in Colorado during the 1980s, when its economy was relatively sick, and moving to New Jersey in 1991, just as Colorado was recovering and New Jersey (and most of the northeastern United States) was sinking quickly into an economic quagmire. In both cases, my job searches and consulting opportunities were somewhat affected by both poor local business prospects and heavy competition from displaced workers (hmmm...maybe it's *me* that's the economic jinx).

Another factor you should understand is the health of the industry in which you've staked your claim. For much of the 1980s, information systems opportunities in the defense and health-care industries were vast. However, with the defense cutbacks that have been going on since the early 1990s, opportunities in that area have dramatically shrunk. It is likely that federally mandated health-care changes will have an opposite effect on I.S. functions in the health-care industry. By assessing and attempting to forecast these types of environmental constraints, you can round out your inventory of factors that will affect your job search.

2.4 Putting It All Together

Once you have begun considering the many areas in which self-assessment is required, it's time to embark on a detailed examination, the goal of which is to establish the ground rules under which your PC-oriented job search will occur. As you might suspect, this should be done whether you are looking for employment in desktop computing (as is the subject matter of our book) or for any other type of position in the computer industry—or in any other industry, for that matter. Books such as *What Color Is Your Parachute?* contain numerous exercises you can do to help you assess your aptitudes, interests, and other factors such as those which we've discussed. They help you determine your strengths and weaknesses, and how to overcome the latter.

For the most part, though, such works are oriented toward the job market and individuals in a general sense, and don't necessarily focus on specific instances except as examples. At the same time, they do a much more thorough job of discussing assessment of personal skills and abilities than we have space to do here and, in cases like *What Color Is Your Parachute?,* have been best-sellers for years.

It is recommended, therefore, that you use one or more of those references for general career and life guidance, and use the material in this chapter for more specific, computer industry–oriented guidance. For example, once you have determined via one of these works that you do indeed wish to remain in the computer industry and that because of the forces discussed in Chap. 1, it is desirable to move your career orientation toward a desktop emphasis, you should then assess the things discussed in this chapter: your career path, functional switches you've made in your career (e.g., hands-on development to hands-off management) and why, and your *computer-specific* strengths and weaknesses. With this information at hand, you can target your job search toward industries, specific technologies, applications areas, and other manageable quadrants instead of being forced to broadcast your résumé and interviewing efforts across an extremely diverse group of companies and organizations, many of which may not even be suitable for you (or at least are places in which you aren't likely to be very happy).

2.5   Chapter Summary

"You can't know where you're going unless you know where you've been."

"I don't know where I'm going, but I'm making good time."

Sayings like these are very applicable to your job search and the interviewing process, whether in general or for desktop computing. Chances are that many of you are in your thirties or forties or older, and—like it or not, fair or unfair—you're at a stage in your career where you can't afford too many false steps as you make changes in employment. This is partly due to the changing employment market in general (lifelong employment is disappearing; there are widespread cutbacks, wage stagnation, etc.), but it is also due to the industry that we all (or most readers at least, I would presume) have chosen for our careers and the changing picture there. Technology marches ahead, and it gets harder and harder for every one of us to stay up to date with what's important and what we need for our jobs, today and tomorrow. Before you embark on trying to build a consulting practice (Chap. 6) in a particular PC-oriented area or retraining yourself for a particular target area in which you want to concentrate your job search, you should be certain that (1) you want to be there, (2) you have the aptitudes and skill set that will increase your chances of success, and (3) all the pieces are in place to help you succeed in both finding what you're seeking and your tasks and roles when you get there.

In the next chapter, we turn our attention to résumés and interviewing, building on our discussion in the first two chapters of the book. Stay tuned.

3

Interviewing, Résumés, and Other Matters

3.1 Introduction

In this chapter, we'll discuss job-hunting activities that you are no doubt familiar with, dating back to your earliest attempts at finding employment. As we'll note, though, the subjects of résumé preparation and interviewing are ones in which there is widespread disagreement among "the experts" as to what is correct and appropriate, and what isn't. Because we're tailoring our discussion to the computer industry, and more specifically to positions related to desktop computing, some of the ambiguity and confusion regarding alternative approaches can be removed; there are certain tacks which have a greater chance of providing you with success than others in this relatively narrow spectrum (as compared with the entire worldwide job market for all industries and all positions), and we'll focus our discussion on these areas.

3.2 Résumés

There is one thing that is certain to drive you absolutely batty when you prepare a new résumé or attempt to update your existing one. You read books (like this one, but dedicated exclusively to résumé preparation), you talk to headhunters and others, and you inevitably will hear the following:

> Make sure that your résumé is in reverse chronological order, with your current or most recent position first. Always base your résumé around your companies and positions, with the various functions you've performed under each position listed in descending order of importance.

Or

> Your résumé should be functional in nature, listing first the functions most pertinent to the position you're seeking and then others, in descending order of how likely they are to be important to that position. At the very end, just list the companies with which you've worked and the dates.

How about

> You should always start off with a statement of your objective, something like "Seeking a supervisory position, specializing in database and CASE technology, where I can positively affect the corporate bottom line."

But

> You should never include a statement of your objectives, because either it will be too general and thus meaningless or, if specific, it is likely to keep you from being considered for any position other than that which you specify as your goal.

Then we have

> List your education first.

Or

> List your education last.

OK, how about

> Always list two or three references.
> Never list references, but always state that references are available on request.
> Never state that references are available on request; that should be obvious.
> Your résumé should never be more than two pages...*Ever!*
> Use as many pages as it takes to successfully market yourself.

One last one:

> List your personal interests, showing what a well-rounded person you are.

But

> Never list personal interests; they have nothing to do with the job. Anyway, suppose you say that you are a Boy Scout leader and the person interviewing you had a horrible experience in the Boy Scouts as a child. You probably won't even be called for an interview.

ARRGGGH! Get the idea? It certainly is enough to cause you serious doubts about which advice to follow, when you can hear or read in different places such divergent directions. And, of course, in any given situation, it's likely that whatever advice you do follow will be wrong. I was once told by a headhunter, when she was reviewing my résumé, that the reverse chronological order I had been using for years was "extremely inappropriate; no hiring manager likes to see that, and he or she will just trash your résumé." Complying with her request, I rewrote my résumé in the functional format she requested (more on each of these later)—for naught, since she never even arranged an interview for me. At a job fair several months later, I handed one of those résumés to a hiring manager at a booth, who grimaced and told me how much he hated functional résumés because it was so hard to learn anything about what someone had done and how he or she had progressed throughout his or her career. He said he liked to see good old chronological order, most recent position first.

So what do you do in these situations? How do you know what preferences the people with screening authority (e.g., those individuals who make the first passes through a stack of résumés to see who should make the first cut) and those who can actually schedule an interview have? While there is no way to be absolutely certain, there are some general guidelines, which we'll discuss in a moment.

Despite the uncertainty raised above with respect to format, there are some definitive rules to the résumé business that you must follow. These are:

First, never, ever lie or exaggerate on your résumé. This includes statements about systems with which you've worked, the level of experience you have, employment dates, companies, positions, educational background, and every other item on your résumé. You may be caught in a lie or an exaggeration immediately, which will automatically remove you from consideration, or your fabrication could be found out after you are hired, and could result in a termination at that point.

All of this is self-explanatory, though. What is more critical to our subject matter in this book is not so much the outright lies as the stretching of sporadic, brief exposures to hardware, software, and communications technologies that you may have had into purported expertise. As we'll discuss later in this chapter, you are very likely to be grilled by at least one interviewer who considers himself or herself an expert in the technical area(s) for which you're being considered. If, say, your résumé states that you have substantial experience with the database product Gupta SQLBase and you're being interviewed for a position that involves extensive use of that product, you will be quizzed about data definition language, data manipulation language, program bindings, file structures, utilities, and numerous other facets of the product. Of course, as we'll discuss later with respect to interviewing, the occasional "I don't know" or "I haven't used that part of the product" is acceptable (or should be, to a reasonable interviewer), but too many of those will cause the interviewer to question the accuracy of your stated claim on your résumé to having substantial experience, and by extension call into question the honesty of your résumé as a whole.

Second, absolutely tailor your résumé to specific job situations and your reading of what the screeners and hiring authorities are likely to be seeking. With word processing capabilities this is a relatively easy process, unlike in the old days, when each version would have to be retyped from scratch.

For example, suppose a position that you're seeking calls for heavy CA-Clipper programming of a variety of business applications, with light design tasks but almost exclusively hands-on programming and development. If your résumé had been prepared in a general manner, you probably would have followed advice such as the following: Always include quantitative accomplishments, such as cost savings, numbers of people supervised or managed, and program revenues.

And, of course, this is fine if you're seeking a managerial position, one with little or no hands-on requirements. For a position such as the development one described above, however, your résumé may in fact work against you if you emphasize your quantitative managerial aspects and downplay your technical accomplishments. This is not to say that you should totally disregard such factors, since in many cases they will be important during the interviewing process in helping to tilt the competition for a position in your favor (in many cases but not all, as we'll discuss shortly). You should, however, recognize that hands-on CA-Clipper skills will be required, and tailor your résumé to emphasize any hands-on experience and accomplishments with that particular product, Xbase systems in general, or applications development as a whole. The accomplishments you should include are things like "developed 60,000-line dBASE III+ system for inventory processing one month ahead of schedule and under allocated budget," perhaps noting things like how the system you developed saved your company (or client, if you did such work in a consulting setting) some number of dollars by improving just-in-time inventory processing or whatever.

It's also important to note what has to be one of the most aggravating paradoxes in the computer job search process. Consider the above example, where a position calls for CA-Clipper development. In many cases, for whatever reasons, experience with another Xbase product (see Chap. 12 for more discussion of PC database products and the Xbase language) such as FoxPro or dBASE IV is not considered adequate experience, and your résumé may not even pass the first screen. It's sort of like saying that if you were an Ada programmer, you would be automatically disqualified from consideration if you had experience with Verdix Ada but not Digital Equipment's VAX Ada. Ridiculous? Actually, you even see compiler-specific requirements in the PC world, such as required experience with Microsoft C; any other C compiler experience you may have is considered inadequate.

While many computer professionals subscribe to the philosophy that a qualified developer who knows several languages or development systems can easily and quickly learn a new language or system simply by studying the documentation and doing some self-initiated experimenting, others hold the belief discussed above that you need to have experience with a specific product, a specific compiler, and a specific system; the marketplace is full of entry-level and displaced people seeking employment or contractual work, so they can afford to be extremely picky. As I discussed in *How to Be a Successful Computer Consultant,* this is an extremely shortsighted view on their part, and often leads to mistakes such as hiring a less qualified person simply because he or she fits some checklist-oriented profile that is heavily influenced by exact matches of specific products and compilers with the experience of those interviewing for a position.

Therefore, with respect to tailoring your résumé, here is some advice that you should follow for the PC marketplace: List all the products with which you have experience, especially if you're seeking a development position. At one time, I would have thought this advice was ridiculous, but after talking with a number of hiring managers and reviewing position announcements and classified and display advertisements, I have come to realize that listing specific products on your résumé may help you pass the first screening. Conversely, the absence of specific products, more often than you would think, can cause your résumé to be eliminated from contention, no matter how qualified you may be or how good a match you are for the position.

This is true not only for products such as FoxPro, CA-Clipper, and dBASE IV, which are development languages and systems in and of themselves, but also for products you wouldn't think to include, such as spreadsheets (Microsoft Excel, Lotus 1-2-3, etc.) and even graphics packages. I was amazed to see how many midlevel positions—not entry-level ones—list job requirements such as "experience with Harvard Graphics and Microsoft PowerPoint" as a plus for the job, or even a job requirement. It honestly seems ludicrous for midcareer professionals, or even entry-level ones, to list the spreadsheets, word processors, and graphics packages with which they have experience; many of you have probably used a hundred or more PC packages. Back in the 1986–1987 time frame, I was working with a consulting company doing a proposal effort for a PC-oriented office information system (OIS), and as part of our proposal generation process, I extensively evaluated nearly every word processing, spreadsheet, database, graphics, and integrated software package that was then on the market. At the time I would have thought it ridiculous to include an item on my résumé that read like the following:

Product Experience:

...

Spreadsheets: Access 20/20, PlanPerfect, Lotus 1-2-3,...

However, quite honestly, that is precisely how some résumé screeners (in my opinion, ill-suited ones) judge your abilities. If the position for which you're sending a résumé involves setting up a LAN-based office information system and the PCs all have Microsoft Excel for spreadsheet functionality, it is quite possible that the absence of the word "Excel" from your résumé will automatically bring a rejection letter.

In some cases, you can get some clue as to what product experience is being sought from reading the advertisement or position announcement, and then tailor your résumé accordingly by making sure that the product(s) and system(s) which will be part of the job's responsibilities are included in your résumé. In other cases, you may have no idea, so a comprehensive list is in order.

Note that an entry like "experience with hundreds of PC and desktop products" will probably not be sufficient, since there are no specific product mentions to catch the screener's attention. When screening hundreds of résumés, one begins to search out a small subset of keywords, and the absence of such keywords (again, fair or not) often causes your résumé to wind up in the rejection pile (or at least the "look at later if we don't find anyone" pile).

Likewise, don't assume that you can deal with product-specific requirements in your cover letter, as very often cover letters do not make it to those technical staff members responsible for screening the résumés; they often receive résumés and little else, and even if they do receive cover letters, they may very well skip right to the résumé.

One unorthodox tack you might consider is annotating your résumé on a case-by-case basis, visually highlighting the product-specific requirements for a given position, as in the following:

Alan Simon
123 Main Street
Smalltown, CT 06060
(203) 555-1212

...

Experience:

XYZ Corporation, 1991–date: Lead Software Developer.

FoxPro for Windows, 25,000 lines	Developed inventory management systems in FoxPro for leading packaged food processing company. Resulting systems reduced inventory holding costs by 25%, and...

U.S. Department of Commerce, 1985–1991: Contract Programmer.

Initially dBASE III+, later ported to FoxPro 2.0	Full life-cycle responsibility for developing export tracking PC-based applications. Implemented 85 node Novell NetWare-based LAN with five servers and five subnets...

University of Connecticut, 1984–1985: Computer Center Analyst.

...

I personally have had good results with annotated résumés tailored to specific job requirements, so this is one idea you may want to seriously consider.

Third, never use the same type of résumé for contract or consulting work as you would for full-time, career-oriented employment. That is especially true if you're going after two different types of employment (e.g., whichever comes first, consulting or full-time, is where you're headed).

Consider that if you do choose to include a career objective near the top of your résumé, a firm looking for consulting or contract PC-related help is not likely to be impressed by a stated objective of "Seeking an organization where I can assume a leadership role and grow throughout my career" or some similar statement which indicates that your preference is for as long an employment period as possible. Rather, such an organization (one seeking consulting help) is likely to focus more on technical abilities and accomplishments that are as close as possible to what their immediate needs are.

Worse, in such a case, regardless of your technical and professional qualifications, any indication that your heart and desires are more with full-time employment than with consulting work may (rightfully) cause a résumé screener to wonder whether you are likely to jump ship from the consulting assignment to the first career-oriented position that comes along, regardless of the state of completion of your project.

One thing I've found useful, having swung back and forth between consulting and corporate life several times during my career, is to have two versions of your résumé always up to date, one oriented toward consulting and contract work (if you are so inclined) and another tailored toward more traditional, climb-the-ladder corporate life. This way, you can increase your options, particularly in the PC marketplace, where opportunities are present in both areas.

Finally, don't put too much emphasis on the mechanics of your résumé. While characteristics like correct spelling, cohesive organization, and visual attractiveness are important, don't assume that things like laser printer output and watermarked high-quality paper are sufficient to overcome technical or professional shortcomings. For the most part, everyone can develop (or have developed for them by a professional résumé writer, although this is discouraged; your résumé should reflect your abilities and strong points, not someone else's perception of them) an attractive résumé, and even if they don't have immediate access to a laser or ink-jet printer at home (which more and more people do these days) or at work (for that after-hours, covert print job!), most professional print shops lease time on PCs so that you can print your résumé and get it copied onto high-quality paper.

Consider, though, that many résumé submissions today are via facsimile machine (FAX) or electronic mail (e-mail), and are likely to wind up in the recipient's hands on whatever print medium he or she has at the office (e.g., glossy FAX paper off of a continuous roll, or dot-matrix print when he or she prints e-mail). Further, in the case of e-mail, the format you specify from a word processing package often isn't preserved during transmission; the basic ASCII text is what is transmitted, not the textual attributes, and the recipient of your résumé via e-mail sees little more than the actual text.

Therefore, while presentation is certainly important for mailed or hand-submitted résumés, don't place too much emphasis on these factors, since in today's job market you probably are going to be pursuing "multimedia" résumé submissions (FAX, e-mail, U.S. mail, etc.).

Again, our focus in these pages is to help you take the general information you no doubt have read about résumés—and the conflicting advice it contains—and place it in the context of our specific subject matter, interviewing for PC- and desktop computing–oriented jobs. Figure 3.1 shows a sample résumé ; you can use this as a guideline as you update or tailor your own. Additionally, the summary at

Bernie C. Jordan
4297 Maple Street
Pittsburgh, PA 15201
(412) 555-0000

Experience Summary

MAJOR MINICOMPUTERS CORPORATION (1987–Present)

Product Manager, Database Systems (5/89–Present)

Product manager for distributed DBMS development effort. Responsibilities include (1) gathering and validating customers' product requirements, (2) marketing the product to internal and external organizations, (3) coordinating pricing, packaging, and scheduling efforts with product and engineering teams, and (4) managing third-party contracted software development effort.

Principal Software Engineer, Database Systems Tools (10/87–5/89)

Responsible for analysis, design, and development of next-generation CASE database management system tools and utilities, as well as investigation and utilization of object-oriented software engineering methodologies and practices. Successfully developed two data modeling tool prototypes. Performed software system integration analysis tasks, including specifying interfaces with other CASE and life cycle support tools. Analyzed competitive CASE tools.

XYZ CONSULTING, INC. (10/86–9/87)

Business Development Manager

Responsible for business development, proposal generation, and hardware/software integration design. Program manager and chief software integration designer for multimillion dollar (>$6 million) PC-based office network for the U.S. Navy Finance Center (2500 users). Managed two multivendor Live Test Demonstrations, one of which included active participation by five firms and equipment/software from fifteen others. Prepared project pro forma cash flow, income, and balance sheet financial statements.

U.S. AIR FORCE, HEADQUARTERS STRATEGIC AIR COMMAND (1982–1986)

Software Design Manager and Ada Prototype Developer (12/85–9/86)

Managed a 10-member development team that designed and engineered a distributed air defense warning system featuring real-time sensor communications, color graphics displays at each workstation, a variety of user interfaces, and large-screen displays.

Chief, Intelligence Systems Communications and Control Section, and Intelligence Communications Programmer (10/82–12/85)

Responsible for designing, developing, and maintaining communications and systems software on one of SAC's major intelligence computer systems. While managing the six-member section, implemented nine new sensor circuits. Duties also included responding to emergencies at SAC HQ.

Figure 3.1 Sample résumé.

COMPUTER CONSULTING SYSTEMS, INC. (1982–Present)

Managing Partner and Founder

Provide microcomputer-based consulting, software, and seminar services to small business firms in Nebraska and Kansas. The three-partner firm, supplemented by subcontract programmers, specializes in database-based information systems for a variety of industries, from telephone communications firms to construction supply companies. Client support and supplemental consulting work continues to date utilizing subcontract assistance as necessary.

NEBRASKA STATE UNIVERSITY (7/82–5/89)

Adjunct Professor

Taught graduate classes in database management systems, computer consulting, and VAX/VMS.

NEW MEXICO STATE UNIVERSITY (1980–1982)

Computer Center Consultant (5/82–10/82)

Responsibilities included database management system evaluation, testing, and prototyping, consulting services for University administrative departments, and analyzing and correcting academic and research community programming problems.

Research Assistant, Management Information Systems (6/81–5/82)

Managed a 10-member programming staff in the implementation of an automated systems analysis/systems design programming set. The automated system was a portion of a continuing multiuniversity research effort into the capabilities and opportunities of computer-assisted information systems design, and was a forerunner of commercial CASE tools.

Teaching Assistant/Instructor, Management Information Systems (8/80–8/81)

Full-charge instructor for a variety of management information systems classes, including COBOL programming, data structures/database management systems, and information systems in society. Responsibilities included planning all lessons, assignments, and examinations, as well as grading all student work.

Education Summary

Master of Science, Management Information Systems, New Mexico State University, College of Business and Public Administration, 1982.   3.83 GPA.
Bachelor of Science, Computer Information Systems, Arizona State University, College of Business Administration, 1980.   3.54 GPA; graduated cum laude.
Numerous professional development and systems-specific training courses.

Publications

Article on real-time systems design, *Computerworld*, September 12, 1985.

Figure 3.1 *(Continued).*

Languages	Systems	Technologies
Ada	DEC VAX Family (VMS, Ultrix)	DBMS: SQL, 4GLs,
COBOL	UNIX workstations (Sun, Counterpoint)	and other query
FORTRAN	Sperry Univac 1100 series (Exec 8)	and programming
Jovial	DEC-10 (TOPS-10)	languages
Basic	CDC Cyber 175 (NOS/BE)	Object-oriented
Univac Assembler	MS-DOS microcomputers	technologies
C	Apple Macintosh microcomputers	Artificial intelligence
Pascal	DEC PDP 11/70 (RSTS/E)	and expert systems
Lisp		CASE
		Systems integration
		and networks

Security Clearance
DoD Secret

Personal Interests
Running, weight lifting, golf, horses, investment finance

Salary History, References, and Personal Background Are Available Upon Request

Figure 3.1 (*Continued*).

the end of this chapter lists a number of sources for advice about résumé preparation that will provide more general guidelines than our admittedly narrow focus here.

3.3 So Where Are the Jobs, Anyway?

Once your résumé issues have been resolved and you have a viable basic résumé which can be quickly tailored to specific situations, your next concern is to target your job search to the areas where you are most likely to be successful. No doubt you've heard statements like

> No one gets a job from the classifieds. Besides, the best jobs aren't advertised in the newspaper.

> You're just wasting your time with headhunters; they're just building up their folder of résumés. Concentrate instead on people you know and their contacts.

And so on. There are some elements of truth to the above statements and others like them (for example, there are probably hundreds of others sending their résumés in response to the same classified ads to which you're responding). What has always puzzled and amused me is the way some people regard multiple job search sources as mutually exclusive. Where is it written that just because newspaper display and classified ads are often a crapshoot, they can't be part of your overall job search effort?

In fact, I would contend that especially in today's computer industry, and particularly because it's likely that you're trying to switch your focus from mainframe or minicomputer technology to PC technology, all of the sources discussed below should be included as part of your effort. On a personal note, in the course of my career, I've received interviews and offers (some of which I've accepted) from organizations found in each of the following ways; at various times one or another has provided a richer source of strong leads, but all have worked at least once.

3.3.1 Advertisements

Whether display or classified ads, whether in the local newspaper (or that of some other city in which your job search is being conducted) or from a national trade periodical like *Computerworld,* you should answer, with a cover letter and résumé, advertisements that sound interesting and that are for positions for which you think you have a good chance to qualify. Sometimes a phone number is given; if so, it's worth calling to achieve "that personal touch" and make yourself known. Other times, you may read "no calls please," and it's recommended that that advice be followed.

Oftentimes you'll read advice that tells you to make as many phone calls as necessary to find out the name of the hiring manager, and call that person directly, bypassing the human resources or personnel department. This advice has some merit, given that your résumé is probably bundled in with hundreds of others. However, having been on the hiring side several times, I can tell you that on a particularly hectic, tough workday, an unanticipated phone call from a job seeker can often be a tremendous irritant, at least on first impulse. I usually try to overcome any personal irritation and focus on that person's gutsy effort, having been involved in job searches myself over the years and having more than once responded to an advertisement that appeared to be tailor-made for me...and never even getting a postcard acknowledgment. There is no guarantee, though, that a hiring manager you contact in such a manner will see that unsolicited contact in the same light, so in my opinion this particular tactic is often a crapshoot. In a tough job market, though, every little bit helps, and you could look at it as, if a bold personal contact would cause a hiring manager to eliminate you from consideration simply for that aggressiveness, you probably didn't want to work for him or her anyway.

3.3.2 Personal contacts

Typically, personal contacts tend to work best when you are searching within a given industry or within a particular technology base. For example, if your experience has been mainly in defense systems, both as a member of the military and as a contractor, you no doubt have a wide network of contacts among defense contractors, and very often this is an excellent way to inquire about and pursue new opportunities. Similarly, if your career has focused almost exclusively on, say, CASE technology and you have spent time working at a CASE tools vendor, you probably have a fairly extensive network in that area—former coworkers who have moved on, people you have met at CASE-oriented conferences, and so on, many of whom can provide you with some solid leads and open doors for you.

I believe, though, that in the PC-oriented industry, particularly for the many of you who are making the transition from careers oriented toward larger systems, this personal network, while still present, is not quite as strong as in the aforementioned cases. For one thing, much of the PC- and desktop-oriented work tends to be done on a solo basis or in small teams, not in groups of dozens or hundreds as might be found on a large defense-oriented software development effort. Therefore, even people who have spent a great deal of time in PC technology often simply haven't worked with as many other people as those from the mainframe or minicomputer worlds.

Also, because of the multifunctional nature of PC-oriented work that we discussed in Chap. 1 (e.g., you often are a software developer, network architect and installer, systems integrator, systems administrator, etc.—all at the same time) and the lack of demarcation among job functions, an individual in this market has less chance to stand out as a "true expert," someone unique who towers above most others. Unlike, say, the SQL-based relational database world, where vendor representatives sit on standards committees, present papers at conferences, and do other high-profile things that are likely to draw attention to their expertise, the PC world offers a limited number of opportunities such as these. It is true, of course, that an expert in a package like FoxPro could go to user's group meetings, attend the Xbase standardization committee (ANSI X3J19) meetings, write articles (e.g., "tips and tricks," product evaluation, etc.) for trade publications, and do other such things to get attention, and these little additions to your repertoire do indeed help. However, for the most part, the typical desktop-oriented developer toils in relative obscurity (for that matter, so does the average mainframe or minicomputer developer) and has fewer channels for technology-based or industry-based job-potential networking than does his or her large-system counter-part.

Again, this is not to knock personal contacts as part of your job search effort, because success in the past often predicts future success, and those who hold you in high regard are often willing to take a chance on you with respect to newer technologies. For those of you who have relied exclusively on that form in the past, though, eschewing all other forms of job searching, it's strongly recommended that you pursue a multipronged approach as you head into the desktop computing industry.

3.3.3   Job fairs

Sometimes job fairs are a total waste of time; other times you come away with a few interview invitations and a job offer or two. It certainly can't hurt to spend a couple of hours when a job fair is in your neck of the woods (or in any other geographical area in which you're interested, for that matter). Most job fairs are multicompany and conducted at a hotel or convention center; others are company-specific, drawing together many different organizations within a large corporation that need computer professionals for their upcoming projects. In both cases, you are likely to find PC-oriented positions available, so go for it!

3.3.4   Recruiters

Ah, headhunters...the scum of the earth, many people would say. And, true, most of us have had some bad experiences with them—or, at the least, a lot of "nonexperiences" in terms of little effort on our behalf, which often makes me wonder just how these folks make any money at all, given that they get paid for placing folks into new companies. In the most recent edition of *How to Be a Successful Computer Consultant,* I described a six-month combination of experimental contacts and actual contract-seeking attempts through consulting-oriented headhunters which would cause anyone to question the work ethic and integrity of most members of that profession.

However, before dismissing all headhunters—some of whom are oriented toward placing full-time employees, others toward consulting placement, and some toward both—from your job search, consider the following:

- There are some good recruiters, people who treat others fairly and make an honest effort to place you in a suitable position.
- It doesn't hurt at all to circulate your résumé among the

recruiters—if nothing comes of it, so be it, but there's always the chance that a lead or two might pop up that will move you into a position using more modern technology.

One thing to note, though, is that recruiters are often trying to specifically match a given skill set with an equally specific set of client requirements, and many times aren't interested in promoting you to a client in the manner of "he (or she) has been an excellent MVS COBOL programmer, and has studied a great deal about dBASE IV programming. I've seen samples of his (or her) work, and he (or she) can certainly fit the bill of what you're seeking." A good recruiter will use (or at least consider) such an approach, but many of the run-of-the-mill ones are simply interesting in matching up someone with, say, Microsoft Excel macro experience with a client specifically looking for that skill set.

Remember, it doesn't hurt to include that channel in your effort.

As a reminder, though, for those of you who have never dealt with recruiters: There are two different types of recruiters, those who are paid by the companies for which they find personnel, and those who charge you to help you with your job search. It is strongly recommended that you concentrate on those who are paid by their client companies, because the last thing you need in the turmoil of looking for a new job and possibly making radical career and lifestyle changes is to be shelling out big bucks with no guarantee that anyone will come through for you.

3.3.5 Online services

Local computer bulletin boards and national information services such as Prodigy and CompuServe have forums in which positions are advertised. Some are directly advertised by hiring companies and others are for recruiters, but all should be studied if you have access to such services.

3.3.6 Intracompany job announcements

Even though most folks who need to make the transition away from technology with shrinking employment prospects (e.g., mainframes) toward desktop computing will find themselves displaced from their current company, some will in fact make the transition within their own company. Most large corporations have intracompany job announcements and bulletins (many also have online job bulletin boards, as discussed above) from which you may learn of PC-related opportunities. Within your current company, you have an advantage over those seeking employment elsewhere, given that personal contacts, performance reviews, and other factors may swing the possibility of job switching your way. While many large companies are determined to reduce headcount, and put internal hiring freezes and similar blocking measures in place in order to either (1) force someone out or (2) set the stage for massive layoffs, others really do put some substance behind their pronouncements about caring for their employees and are willing to help you make the transition into more modern technologies. If you like the company for which you currently work and you have an opportunity to make the technology transition within those confines, this arguably should be your primary focus in your job search. Note that this doesn't make you immune from the interviewing process; you still need to go through that.

3.3.7 Consulting-oriented business development

In Chap. 6 we'll discuss the mechanics of consulting as a stopgap measure, a way to fill the void until you either find full-time employment or complete a retraining program. As part of the computer consulting process, you need to find clients, and we'll expand on the items discussed above with respect to consulting.

3.4 Interviewing

OK, once again, to reiterate the opening salvo of this book, all together now...interviewing stinks.

Now, with that out of the way, let's get down to the heart of the matter. You have to go through the interviewing process. There is almost no way around it (occasionally you hear of the rare unsolicited, out-of-the-blue offer before an interview is conducted, but these situations are indeed rare), and it is critical that you get across the correct message to those who have the authority to hire you, as well as those who have input into that process.

As with résumés, there are many different books that give you advice about interviewing, and some of these are cited at the end of this chapter. Rather than go through common, general advice (wear a suit, be on time, research the company, etc.), we'll focus our discussion in this section on information that is specifically oriented toward helping you make the transition into desktop computing.

Very often, your first interview contact with a prospective employer will be by telephone during a phone screen. Sometimes the person on the other end may be from human resources or personnel; on other occasions he or she may be a hiring manager or a potential coworker. Regardless of whom you speak with or how long the conversation is, don't underestimate that contact because it is the gateway to your opportunity to present your qualifications in person. If you treat the phone contact too casually, your opportunity may well be lost.

Likewise, whether over the phone or during an in-person interview, try to present your information and answer questions in just the right form. Obviously, dry, uninspired answers delivered in a monotone will detract from your presentation, regardless of how technically astute you may be. On the other side of the spectrum, however, remember that you're in an interview, not at happy hour. Anecdotes that describe your problem-solving abilities, technical insight, and other assets are fine and should be presented whenever possible, but consider the two following ways in which the same material is presented:

Question from an interviewer: "Give us an example of where you had to solve a difficult technical problem, and the approaches you took to accomplish that."

Answer #1:

> There was an occasion where the communications software for which I was responsible apparently malfunctioned, but there was nothing in the dump that indicated where the problem was because all of the registers had been corrupted by the abnormal termination. To run the debugging facility for our communications modules, we typically had to be in live, test-mode contact with the remote site, and the next comm test run wasn't scheduled until about two weeks later. During the time that we were analyzing the problem and trying to find any bugs in the code, it occurred again, and the CIO was getting pretty upset.
>
> I recommended that we take one of the other processes in the system—we had a multiprocess environment—and modify its code to dump the message that had caused the problem into the common area buffers and simulate the external communications interrupt, and all of our debugging facilities could be on. We tried this and it worked, and we found the problem later that day and fixed it immediately.

Answer #2:

> We had this communications problem with one of our lines. I'm sitting in the office trying to get some things done and the operations controller calls me and tells me that the comm line blew up the entire system. So this kid, maybe nineteen, twenty years old, a college co-op student, I think, is sweating bullets because the entire system is down and the next thing is that the CIO is going to get called at home during dinner, you know? So I calm him down and walk him through the entire thing and I figure out that yeah, it's the comm line, but when this kid ships

the dump down to me, there's absolutely nothing there that I can use to figure out the problem. You ever see one of those XYZ vendor dumps? Man, they're horrible, like something out of the stone age; Fred Flintstone probably debugged his software that way, you know?

So anyway, this problem happens again and we can't get a live test until 2 weeks later—the guys at the remote site are being hard-...I mean, difficult about the problem, really not team players, you know? So I go to the CIO's deputy and I tell him that we don't need those remote site guys, I know how we can get this thing done and figure out the problem. This guy, two, maybe three years out of college, he can't really make up his mind, so I tell him, "Let me talk to the CIO now" and I get in and present my idea. The CIO loves it and we run the test—oh, yeah, I faked out the communications interrupt by popping a message in the buffer from another process and simulating the interrupt—and what do you know, there's the problem, plain as day in front of us. So I....

Well, I'm sure you get the idea. Your answers should be right to the point, emphatic and narrative, yet not dry, but not like you're at the local bar, discussing the softball team's game and your great play at shortstop and that double to left-center.

As in your résumé, you should avoid any exaggerations and outright falsehoods; don't bluff, because you will be found out. For example, if you have claimed to be a dBASE III+ and dBASE IV expert (or at least to have extensive development experience), you can expect questions like

- What are some of the major differences between dBASE III+ and dBASE IV?

- Did you convert any programs from dBASE III+ to dBASE IV? What problems did you encounter?

- How many database files can you have open at the same time in dBASE IV?

- How many index files can you have open for each database file in dBASE III+?

- What does the STRING() function do? Can you give me an example?

- How would you solve [some small application problem] using dBASE IV?

And so on. Don't assume that, say, you can bluff your way into a CA-Clipper position in which experience with that product is required through your knowledge of dBASE or FoxPro, unless you do extensive study and understand the similarities and differences among the products in great detail (and even then you're likely to be tripped up). This doesn't mean that you can't get a CA-Clipper position on the basis of your dBASE experience, just that you shouldn't try to pass yourself off as having certain experience that you don't have. Many technical interviewers love to grill you about your experience with their favorite products or systems, and if an interviewer is himself or herself an expert, he or she will be able to spot exaggerations and fabrications on your part with relative ease.

Even for areas with which you have a great deal of experience, you should tailor your answers to the type of person with whom you're interviewing at that moment. Let's take the above example, in which you're looking for a PC database programming position (regardless of which product is in use at the company with which you're interviewing). In interviewing sessions with technically oriented peers (e.g., potential future coworkers), your conversations may very well focus on specific product features, product version differences, trade-offs between two alternative means of doing the same function (e.g., "What are the differences between SEEK and FIND in dBASE III+?"), and similar areas that are designed to permit the interviewer(s) to discover your specific technical knowledge. If you see that the conversation is headed in this direction, you should focus your answers squarely on the technologies in question.

On the other hand, many hiring managers (especially if you are looking for a consulting position and are interviewing with a business owner who is primarily a computer user rather than an information systems professional) will focus their questions on your problem-solving abilities, creativity, tenacity ("stick-to-it-ness"), and proficiency at using your technical skills to solve business problems. They may be less interested in, say, the difference between DISPLAY and LIST in dBASE III+. However, you can still demonstrate your technical proficiency by statements such as the following:

> On the system I set up at ABC Corp., the original versions didn't use any index files because they were on old IBM PC-XTs with limited disk space, and the overhead of maintaining the index structures would have required ABC to buy an external drive, which wasn't cost-effective. Instead, they ran their long reports that had to be sorted over the weekend, since they were batch-oriented in nature. However, when I upgraded the system in 1989, they upgraded their hardware and we examined the possibility of adding index structures to the database environment. There was now plenty of room and they were beginning to want more and more of their reports real-time instead of by weekend batch, so we upgraded the software at that time and added new ad hoc reporting capabilities....

Again, just as with a speech or presentation, you should understand and know something about your audience, and adjust your remarks so that they are likely to be most effective in stressing your qualifications to the individual(s) with whom you are speaking at any one time.

On a final note, it's important to understand that in attempting to make the transition to the desktop computing world from whatever your background is, don't oversell the wonders of PCs, workstations, client/server computing, and the like. Avoid statements like, "There won't be any mainframes left in five years; they'll all be replaced by client/server systems like the ones you have here at XYZ Corp. because of the tremendous cost savings." (Oh? most of corporate America and federal, state, and city government agencies would disagree that the mainframe is dead; careers in those technologies may be stagnating somewhat, and desktop technologies and systems based on PCs and LANs are growing in numbers and importance, but the data center will probably remain in the grasp of the mainframe forever. Also, most implementations of client/server computing as mainframe replacements show little in the way of cost savings.) You can easily discuss "the wonders of PCs" and your abilities with those systems without blanket statements such as the one above that call into question your overall understanding of and insight into multiple levels of information systems technology.

3.5 Corporate Loyalty

As part of the "other matters" component of this chapter's title, I'd like to say a few words about corporate (or organizational, for those of you in the government world) loyalty, specifically in the context of job searching. Many observers of career-related matters (myself included) agree that the days of lifelong employment within the same company are dwindling rapidly; one only needs to look at the layoff-of-the-day announcements that, with only a few brief periods of interruption, have been going on since 1990—2000 layoffs here, 5000 layoffs there, 85,000 total job cuts at IBM. This will keep going on for a while, especially in *Fortune* 500–class corporate America.

As you seek employment, most likely within a new company, you may have something of a bitter taste because of your current (or most recent) job situation. Perhaps you were laid off, or are about to be, not because of poor performance, but simply because you were in the wrong place at the wrong time. Your company may even be announcing record profits and the senior executives pocketing seven-digit (or larger) bonuses, but for whatever reason, you're hitting the bricks, possibly in mid-career, desperately trying to transform your skill set into something marketable.

I personally am no fan of corporate America or of large bureaucracies like government agencies, and I've come to believe that with few exceptions, those of us outside the executive suite and the boardroom are little more than interchangeable cogs. I firmly believe that individuality, or at least teamwork on a small-scale basis (e.g., in a small company), is the wave of the future, at least if you want to be rewarded adequately for your successes and contributions.

Even though there's a good chance—a very good chance—that the place in which your current job search ends will not be your employer for more than a couple of years and that this won't be your last job search, I firmly believe that while you are in the employ of a company, you do owe that firm your best efforts and honest dealings. It is easy to be bitter about being on the receiving end of job cuts while executives receive compensation that often is far in excess of their individual contributions to the company's successes, and if you see such history about to repeat itself at the company in which you find yourself, then by all means take preventive and proactive steps like those discussed in this book instead of waiting for the ax to fall. While you're at your new place of employment, though, treat it as a new start. Be loyal to that place as long as you are being treated well, and don't assume that what has happened in the past will automatically happen again.

3.6   It's a Small World, After All...

And finally, keep in mind that it is indeed a small world, even if you are making a transition out of a cliquish career path (e.g., "the database professionals" or "the Beltway bandit defense contractors") where many people know one another across corporate lines. Even in the rather dispersed PC-oriented world, it is common to know someone who knows a former coworker or your former boss. While this can be good from the personal contact side, giving you a bit of networking ability in an area where it is often lacking (as we discussed earlier), you need to be careful about denigrating others, either intentionally (which of course you should never do, whether during an interview or when discussing your former company and supervisor) or through a slip of the tongue.

Situation: You have been hired by AAAAA Corp. as a PC office automation specialist, and it's your first week. You're eating lunch with your new coworkers, and someone asks how things had been at ZZZZZ Inc., your former employer. You talk about the idiotic management decision by your former boss that cost your company market share and led to layoffs, and it turns out that one of your coworkers used to work for your former ZZZZZ Inc. manager several companies ago, and what do you know, they live down the street from one another and belong to the same church and sing in the choir together and....

Oops! Remember that it's best to keep remarks on the positive side or, when discussing negative subjects, to keep your tone nonpersonal and neutral (for example, in the above situation, "We tried adding entity-relationship modeling to our CASE tool a couple of years ago, but the market window for basic E-R functionality had already passed us by, and we didn't do so well in the marketplace because most of our competitors already had extensions to their modeling techniques").

3.7 Chapter Summary

In this chapter, we've focused on the major subjects that are likely to be of critical importance to you, either immediately or in the near future. Again, as we noted in the previous chapter, it's important that you have a good feel for where you're headed with respect to your career directions and personal situation, and the self-assessment process we discussed in Chap. 2 is crucial before proceeding with the steps in this chapter.

Once you have a firm grasp on your situation and where you need and want to head, you need to develop a résumé (several variations, actually) designed to attract the attention of first-line screeners and hiring managers and bring you personal interviews. There are several different channels you can use in seeking your next employment, and it is recommended that you pursue all of them in parallel with one another.

And finally, once you secure that coveted interview, have a game plan when you go in. Know the types of things you're going to say to different types of interviewers (e.g., potential coworkers vs. a nontechnical hiring manager), keep the tone professional yet casual (don't be uptight, but remember that it isn't a happy hour conversation), and in general follow the basic interviewing guidelines that you will find in the references cited below.

Further information about résumé preparation, job searching, and interviewing

Carol Carter, *Majoring in the Rest of Your Life*, The Noonday Press, New York, 1990, and *Graduating Into the '90s*, The Noonday Press,

New York, 1993. Both books are oriented toward younger college-age and postcollege professionals, and have numerous tips and anecdotes about job-related matters, résumés, and so on.

John E. McLaughlin and Stephen K. Merman, *Writing a Job-Winning Resume*, Prentice-Hall, Englewood Cliffs, N.J., 1990.

Richard Nelson Bolles, *What Color Is Your Parachute?*, Ten Speed Press, Berkeley, Calif., published annually. One of the most often-referenced sources of self-insight and job-related matters, this book is must reading for anyone who doesn't want to bounce around aimlessly from job to job (or continue doing so).

Note that *Majoring in the Rest of Your Life* lists other reference sources about career-related matters, and a trip to any mall book store or book superstore will yield a bonanza of reading material.

4

Retraining Yourself
for a New Marketplace

4.1 Introduction

So now you know where you're headed, or at least where you want to go, with your career, because you've conducted an honest, insightful self-assessment of your current skill set and your aptitudes. As part of that exercise, you should have a pretty good idea of your strengths and weaknesses.

As you've been going through the résumé and interview process, you may very well have found companies where the hiring manager and other interviewers are extremely impressed with your abilities and past accomplishments, and are willing to give you assistance with your transition into desktop computing technology by providing you with a formal training program. They'll teach you, say, FoxPro and Microsoft Access development either through an in-house course or by sending you to a seminar or training session conducted by an outside source. Once you've completed this training, you'll be ready to go in your new job.

Suppose, though, that in these days of corporate cost cutting, your lack of current knowledge about the specific PC products and development platforms in use at a company becomes a tremendous barrier to finding employment there. I will be the first to argue that if you can write IMS or IDMS database programs (hierarchical and network data models, respectively), you *certainly* can write FoxPro applications, but interestingly enough, there are many people with hiring authority who either (1) don't have the budgets for training of staff or (2) can't make the association between complementary technologies because of a lack of knowledge or for some other reason.

Fortunately, you're in one of the few industries where you can, very likely *on your own,* upgrade your own skills and overcome these barriers. In this chapter we'll discuss how you can retrain yourself for the desktop computing marketplace, giving yourself the experience that you may not have had the opportunity to receive through a formal workplace setting but nonetheless is within your grasp.

4.2 How I Did It

I know you didn't buy this book to read my autobiography, but since I did exactly what I'm describing in this chapter more than a decade ago (I was ahead of my time, I guess), I'd like to take a few brief paragraphs to tell you how I personally made the transition to PC-oriented skills and, I believe, greatly aided my own career in the computer field.

Like nearly all graduates of computer curricula in the 1970s and early 1980s, my academic experience had been on mainframe and minicomputer systems, through both terminal-based timesharing and using punched cards. As a senior at Arizona State University, I had worked at the Arizona attorney general's office as a programmer/analyst, using the same Sperry Univac (now Unisys) 1100/42 mainframe system that I used at ASU (we leased dial-up time from the campus computer center).

Following graduate school, where my on-line experience was still mainframe- and minicomputer-based, I entered the Air Force in 1982, only to find that my assignment was as a communications and systems programmer for a Sperry Univac 1100/42-based system, in a language known as JOVIAL. Despite being relatively sophisticated for a language developed in the late 1950s, with enumerated types and block statements, the plain fact was that outside of the defense industry (and more specifically Air Force systems), JOVIAL was almost unheard of. Further, the 1100/42 systems were aging, and even though newer members of that family were available (such as the 1100/72), I was a bit worried about my marketability four years later, when my Air Force commitment was to expire.

Further cementing my career-oriented concern was the boom in PC technology, which was just starting to hit its stride in 1982. Our Air Force office didn't receive our first PC until mid-1983, and microcomputers were sparse around military offices.

Along with my desire to begin consulting part-time for additional income and greater career path options, I felt it was to my advantage to learn something about PC technology, and so I purchased an Osborne portable computer (the one with the tiny screen, for those of you who remember those systems) which came bundled with word processing, spreadsheet, and database packages (WordStar, SuperCalc, and dBASE II, respectively).

Now in general I've never been one to play with computers outside the context of business or a job, but in the context of personal finances, recordkeeping, letter writing, and other functions, I extensively used each of the packages that came with the system. I wrote a number of dBASE II recordkeeping applications, including a double-entry accounting system and a periodical tracking package.

When a local personal computer retailer advertised in the paper for consultants willing to do application development, I was able to go in and, armed with my knowledge of dBASE II, work with the retailer on a proposal for a client. We won that competitive effort. dBASE III came out just as the project was starting, and I self-taught myself dBASE III based on my knowledge of the previous version. I continued doing work for that client for seven years and was able to build on that experience to win other business, and we all lived happily ever after.

That's enough about me; the point is that more than a decade ago, before anyone envisioned PCs becoming viable corporate computing platforms, before anyone had heard the term *client/server,* I was concerned about my career viability and took a *proactive* approach towards teaching myself the skills that I thought would be beneficial to my career. Let's now switch our focus to what *you* can do *today* to accomplish the same feat.

4.3 It Don't Come Easy, You Know It Don't Come Easy

The absolute first thing you must do is come to terms with the fact that retraining yourself will not be an easy process. Or, at least, it won't be *effortless,* since you may be pleasantly surprised how naturally PC technology comes to you, but even if you have a natural aptitude for PC-oriented skills, it *will* take a great deal of work to accomplish your goal.

Fortunately, you're in one of the few professions where you can actually retrain yourself, on your own time and on your own terms (e.g., schedules, pace, where you target your efforts, etc.). Further, you can accomplish this retraining with a minimal investment, as we'll discuss next.

4.4 Buy a Computer...Maybe Two!

Suppose for a moment that you were an aerospace engineer specializing in military fighter aircraft. Given the trends in military weapons spending, you naturally would be worried about your long-term job prospects. To retrain yourself for a new line of work, whether a variant of your current work in engineering or something in another career area, you would probably have to return to school to pursue a new educational path, and even then your newly acquired experience wouldn't be "real world," but rather academic in nature.

In the past, when mainframes were the norm and "personal computing" didn't exist, there was little or no way to give yourself hands-on experience in a cost-effective manner. Say that you were a Honeywell GCOS mainframe programmer, and you wanted to learn IBM 370 systems. Short of paying for a class or training course which would offer only a limited amount of hands-on systems time, you would have to study on your own from books about DOS/VSE and other operating systems, JCL, PL/I, etc., and your acquired knowledge would be primarily theoretical, rather than cemented through extensive hands-on usage.

In today's computer industry, though, you have a tremendous advantage over your predecessors as you move your skills base to the desktop arena. For a relatively small amount of money, you can buy (1) a fairly powerful personal computer, (2) a supporting systems software environment, (3) applications development systems, and even (4) rudimentary networking hardware and software. Let's look at this in more detail.

4.4.1　Your PC

Many of you already have a home personal computer, which you probably use for basic recordkeeping, game playing, tracking financial assets, and other functions. If you purchased your system in recent years and have a reasonably powerful and high-capacity system (as discussed below), you can easily use that system for your personal retraining program. If, however, you still are working predominantly with an 80286 (PC AT class) system with an older version of DOS, no Microsoft Windows, a limited amount of memory and disk capacity, and other limitations, then perhaps it's time to move into "training class" hardware, as we'll discuss next. The same is true for those of you who are using older Apple Macintosh systems with pre-System 7 operating systems and similar memory and storage capacity limitations.

For now, let's focus our examples on "traditional" personal computers, those based on Intel microprocessors (386, 486)—the family of systems that used to be commonly referred to as "IBM PC compatible." Later, we'll expand our discussion to other types of systems, depending on your specific personal training goals.

Today (i.e., as I'm writing this), you can purchase an i486 system with 8 megabytes of memory, over 200 megabytes of disk storage, and a fairly decent color monitor for between $1000 and $2000, depending on the specific type of processor (e.g., SX, DX, or DX2), the clock speed, and other variables. In short, for roughly $1200 or so you can give yourself a platform on which you can train yourself for pretty much everything you'll need to learn about that branch of the desktop computing world: software development, basic networking skills, graphical user interface (GUI) usage and development, software installation and configuration, and basic systems administration.

As noted in the section heading, you may very well want to consider purchasing *two* computers, particularly if you want to really get some hands-on experience with various networking hardware and software products. With, say, two 486-based systems, one perhaps more powerful and with greater memory and disk capacity than the other, you can set up a small two-station local area network (LAN) and teach yourself things like loading protocol drivers, configuring and managing a user base (user IDs, permissions, etc.), troubleshooting, and other such subjects.

The above pattern applies to other desktop computing areas in which you want to train yourself for future opportunities: Apple Macintosh (68xxx-based systems) computers, various other 68xxx-based systems running variants of desktop UNIX (discussed next), PowerPC systems, Alpha-based PCs, etc. While prices certainly increase as you add more power and capacity to your training systems, the nice thing is that for the most part, computers at reasonable prices can often function as surrogates for more powerful, more expensive models. That is, you can teach yourself how to do Microsoft Windows programming on a reasonably priced 486 SX system, and the skills you learn will be directly applicable to 486 DX2, 66-MHz systems that cost somewhat more. Even if prospective jobs or consulting projects will involve "souped-up" high-capacity systems, skills learned on reasonably priced training systems will be applicable there as well.

Finally, there is no reason to limit yourself to only one type of hardware as part of your training program. If you have committed yourself to purchasing two systems to learn LAN technology, you could perhaps purchase a 486 Windows system *and* a Macintosh System 7 computer, and tie the two together in a network configuration. Not only will you have two different platforms on which you can practice (for example, if you learn GUI development on both Windows and System 7, you can cement your understanding of the basic concepts behind GUIs by seeing the similarities between the application architectures on these two systems), but you can also teach yourself about heterogeneous environments and communications among systems in such environments; given that heterogeneity is just as important and dominant a trend in computing as downsizing is, this will give your job prospects an added boost.

4.4.2   Systems software

You absolutely, positively, must use your hardware training platform to teach yourself the following skills:

Graphical user interfaces (GUIs).   Not only *using* GUIs (for those of you who have operated exclusively in block or character terminal environments in the past), but also being able to *develop* GUI software is critical. Desktop applications invariably involve a GUI, such as Microsoft Windows in the traditional PC marketplace, the Macintosh toolbox (the first widely used GUI, introduced in 1984), and to a lesser extent X Windows (for desktop UNIX environments).

Note that you don't necessarily need to be able to develop GUI applications from scratch, that is, using all of the native services available for windows and menu management, different types of dialog boxes (e.g., modal and nonmodal; see Chap. 9), mouse and keyboard drivers, and so on. In many cases, you will find yourself using development software through which application programming interfaces (APIs) to the underlying native GUI system will provide you with some degree of abstraction from the tedium of GUI development. That is, instead of having to code main event handler routines which service keyboard and mouse interrupts, you may use a system such as MacApp for Apple Macintosh applications or FoxPro for Windows for Microsoft Windows database applications, in which you manage such basic functionality through higher-level function calls that are provided by the systems (Fig. 4.1).

The key to learning how to do GUI development, in whatever form and on whatever platform you choose, is to practice, practice, and practice even more. Create dozens or hundreds of screen mockups (perhaps using underlying program stubs, or maybe doing "real work" underneath). You should learn how to handle mouse and keyboard events, how to create menus and submenus; how to provide modal (synchronous) and nonmodal (asynchronous) dialog boxes; how to use radio buttons, list boxes, and other types of information-gathering agents within dialog boxes and on menus; and other basic control functions. Further, you should learn how to do basic graphics handling, such as line drawing, object movement and resizing, text management (attribute definitions, such as color, size, and font; text cre-

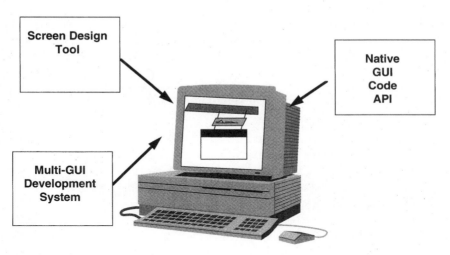

Figure 4.1 GUI development using abstraction platforms.

ation; text editing and manipulation; etc.), and whatever else you can possibly learn.

PC-oriented database skills.   Many of you from the mainframe and minicomputer worlds have had little or no exposure to database and database management system (DBMS) technology, focusing instead on VSAM and other file structures as your primary data management environments. Many others of you that do have database skills have focused exclusively on hierarchical (e.g., IBM's IMS) or network (e.g., Computer Associates' CA-IDMS) products. *Products based on the relational model dominate the PC world* (although it is inevitable that object-oriented databases will gain more prominence there in upcoming years, as well). Note that I say "products based on the relational model" instead of "relational PC database products," because in the purest sense (e.g., according to the defining model of relational data management, Dr. E. F. Codd's 1970 paper), PC products aren't truly relational in terms of following all of the mathematical properties of the model. But—and this is very important—*the user community for PC databases doesn't care!* While many in academia and even in industry focus on such issues as conformance to "the real relational model," this is of little or no importance to the departments and small business organizations that are most likely to base an information system around CA-Clipper or FoxPro. And so herein lies another hint for your interviewing process: *Never,* during an interview for a position involving development work with PC databases, make off-hand remarks referring to products such as FoxPro or Paradox for

Windows as "not really being DBMS," or pontificate on these products' shortcomings in transaction management compared with mainframe or large-system products with which you are familiar. You are likely to be dismissed as being too theoretical or too "computer science–intensive" for an environment in which major advantages for a product are factors such as development tools, prototyping capabilities, usability, and similar user-oriented facilities.

Local area network (LAN) skills.   At one time, PCs were primarily stand-alone office productivity machines, used for word processing, *personal* file management, and small, single-user (or at least one user at a time) applications. In today's environments, at least the kind in which you are likely to find yourself pursuing employment, most information systems involve at least some degree of local area networking tying systems together, with one or more servers providing file, database, and other services to users' desktops in a client/server configuration. Therefore, to be competitive in the desktop computing market, you have to be able to not only utilize the information management environments (e.g., the PC and desktop database products) and user interfaces, but also enable applications or components of applications to communicate with one another or with system services at remote locations.

To do this, your applications—and your training program to teach you how to develop those applications—should call network services such as those available in Novell NetWare and be able to access and communicate with remote systems. If your personal training environment involves two different computers, you can configure one to function as a file or database server and the other to be a NetWare client system and learn how to write client/server applications of the type you are likely to find yourself writing in the PC marketplace.

Development software.   Many developers—from mainframe environments in particular, but from minicomputer environments as well—have experience primarily with 3GLs such as COBOL or PL/I or with assembly language. Further, as we noted earlier, assignments in these types of environments tend to be more specialized in nature, focusing exclusively on user interfaces, data management, or other areas (including the main applications processing).

In desktop computing environments, a substantial portion of the development is done using 4GLs, screen and forms generators, CASE-based code generators, and similar systems that are geared toward higher development productivity at the expense of low-level, highly detailed capabilities such as those needed to write communications protocol drivers. (Of course, desktop development is also done using 3GLs—particularly C—or even in assembly language, and 4GLs and code generators are also found on mainframes and minicomputers; you are likely, though, to encounter this development paradigm shift as you make the transition into a PC environment.)

Further, in desktop environments you are more likely to find yourself using multiple developmental systems (different 4GLs, some C or Pascal, different screen generators, etc.), so your personal training system should include those products that you believe you are most likely to encounter. Additionally, as we'll discuss shortly, you need to make a concerted effort to stay up to date with new "hot" products and technologies, new product releases, etc.

4.4.3   Applications software

In the desktop world, some degree of software development is done using products that are primarily classified as applications software. For example, software packages such as Microsoft Excel or Lotus 1-2-3, used primarily for spreadsheet management, have rather complex macro languages in which applications, complete with user dialogs and sophisticated conditional processing, can be created. Additionally, advanced product features such as spreadsheet cell locking are often directed more toward professional developers than toward the user community.

Other packages, such as Lotus Notes, have some degree of complexity for which full-time development and systems management is necessary. Therefore, your training system should permit you to develop expertise with a number of popular applications packages that the success of your job search may require.

4.5   Formal Training

In addition to home-based self-training—which is most important to your interviewing success and job acquisition because of the intensive, real-world practice that you can provide yourself—you may want to consider adding formal training such as seminars, classes, and courses to your retraining process. You may want to take a four-day course in, say, Paradox for Windows or Visual Basic, in which you receive instruction and guidance as well as hands-on practice.

It is strongly recommended, though, that you follow up any formal training with steady work on your own system, otherwise your knowledge is likely to wither with disuse.

4.6   Staying Current

Once your retraining program has been completed and you feel confident that you can compete for desktop computing positions, it's important to ensure that your skills and knowledge stay up to date, even after you have found a new job. Remember that one of the reasons you are making a transition to desktop computing skills under rather trying circumstances is that for whatever reasons (including those beyond your control), your knowledge and experience with newer information systems technology has fallen behind that of others. You want to prevent a recurrence of this displacement, and therefore it's recommended that you stay up to date as much as possible with new products, new versions of products you use or have used in the past, and technology in general.

For example, suppose you first made the transition to the PC world in the mid-1980s, focusing on dBASE III and dBASE III+ development. If you haven't done much work in the PC database area since the late 1980s, you need to catch up on

- dBASE IV (new product version)

- FoxPro, CA-Clipper, dbFast, and other such products (other Xbase language products that are widely used)

- Microsoft Windows versions of products like FoxPro and Paradox (GUI enhancements to traditional PC development systems)

- Microsoft Access (another Microsoft Windows product, but different technology)

The same need to stay current is present in the hardware world as well, with newer generations of popular PC processors (e.g., i486 DX2, Pentium), new processors (Alpha, PowerPC), disk drive technology, connectivity among different processor types, etc. Systems software, applications packages—it doesn't matter what area of computer technology, you had better stay as up to date as possible to remain competitive in the job market.

In both *How to Be a Successful Computer Consultant* and *The Computer Professional's Survival Guide,* there are chapters that deal with how to stay current with the massive overload of business and technical subjects that are important to your career. Briefly, I advocate a "just-in-time" approach in which you subscribe to a broad range of periodicals (many of them available at no cost) that cover a wide range of subjects—in this particular case, especially those that deal with desktop computing technology—and skim as many articles as possible, the goal being to have a cursory understanding of as many subjects as possible. At the point a particular product or technology becomes important to you (say for a job interview or to compete for a position at work), you should have a general understanding of that subject from your periodic study; you can then immerse yourself in it and learn as much as possible in a relatively short period.

For example, if you are a database professional who has concentrated primarily on Xbase systems (dBASE IV, FoxPro, etc.), you should at least be familiar with the basic product functionality and capabilities of Microsoft Access. You may have learned this from reading product reviews in a magazine such as *Data Based Advisor,* even though you have never used the product.

At the point when Microsoft Access experience becomes important to you—perhaps when interviewing for a new job or for a consulting project—you can then pursue the immersion part of keeping up to date, which would include

- Going back through your own personal library and rereading articles and reviews about the product, including some you may have just cursorily skimmed the first time around

- Conducting on-line, keyword-based searches (for example, through CompuServe) and downloading as many recent articles as possible

- Ordering demonstration copies of software

- Purchasing a copy of the product for your home system so that you can get hands-on experience

From this immersion effort, you can learn about product facilities and how to use them, tips and tricks, workarounds for any shortcomings, etc.

4.7 Chapter Summary

Retraining yourself for anything, including desktop computing technology, requires tremendous effort on your part. You must first come to grips with the fact that just because the computers are smaller and easier to use than those which you may have used in the past, this does not minimize your need to learn about new hardware, systems and applications software, networking technology, developmental paradigms, etc.

Further, no one else can accomplish the retraining for you. Even if you attend formal training courses, you will do most of the learning on your own. This will involve long hours, and often a great deal of frustration and bewilderment, but once you have empowered yourself and through your own determination and effort have brought your skills base to the point when you can successfully compete in today's computer job market, you are ready to conquer any challenge that any new position will bring.

5

What's Hot Today...
and What Will Be Hot
Tomorrow

5.1 Introduction

Lest you get the idea from our discussion in earlier chapters that the multifunctional nature of most positions in the desktop computing world means that (1) most jobs are nearly identical to one another and (2) computer professionals in this environment wind up doing everything that there is to do, it should be understood that despite the broad base of skills and expertise required, there is still some degree of specialization present in most positions. Whether it is specializing in certain types of applications or working primarily in client/server environments, the characteristics of "good" jobs vary from those of run-of-the-mill or dead-end positions.

In this chapter, we'll discuss some of the areas in the desktop computing world that are particularly promising with respect to opportunities in both today's and tomorrow's environments. These areas are listed in Fig. 5.1, but it should be noted that the dynamic nature of information systems technology undoubtedly means that, say, two years from now, this list of hot areas may well vary from that of today, and thus you should revisit it as part of your career planning activities.

5.2 New Hardware

Way back in the early days of PCs—the late 1970s and early 1980s—there were a number of different branches in the road down which PC

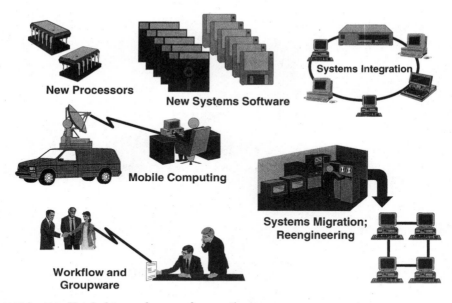

Figure 5.1 Hot desktop and personal computing areas.

technology was heading; the Apple II family, powered by Motorola microprocessors; CP/M machines, with Z80 or Intel 8080 chips; Radio Shack TRS-80 systems; and, of course, the IBM PC and its compatibles.

In the mid-1980s, a shakeout occurred in the PC market, and, for the most part, only two major PC hardware alternatives remained: IBM PC compatibles, which made up the majority of desktop systems, and the Apple Macintosh family. Because of the convergence of the marketplace on these two types of systems, and because of the growing legions of PC-literate computer professionals (and even sophisticated end users), proficiency with either of these types of systems was no longer a great differentiator of one's skills and suitability for a particular position. Even the workstation world—the more powerful desktop alternatives to PCs—was dominated by a select few systems (Sun MicroSystems and others who produced SPARC systems, Digital Equipment VAXStations, many vendors' systems based on the MIPS RISC chip, IBM's RS/6000, etc.), and for the most part those workstations ran some variant of the UNIX operating system, so that differentiating one's skills from those of others was difficult in the workstation arena as well.

Today, however, the desktop hardware market is diverging again, leading to new opportunities to differentiate yourself from competitors for jobs and consulting projects. Digital Equipment's Alpha processor; the PowerPC chip from Apple, Motorola, and IBM; Intel's Pentium—there is a strong likelihood that an organization pursuing desktop computing with one or more of these systems will lack sufficient expertise among its current staff and will have to hire or contract for the skills it requires. Therefore, one way to differentiate yourself so that you first get interviews and then win a position is to be proficient in emerging hardware technology that is likely to be popular in the marketplace.

5.3 New Systems Software

Along with hardware technology, systems software—operating systems, operating environments, developmental platforms—is diverging from the somewhat static PC marketplace of recent years, dominated by DOS, Microsoft Windows, and Apple Macintosh System 7 (with some UNIX presence through products like SCO* Open Desktop). Systems such as Microsoft Windows NT, NextStep (on non-Next platforms, given the company's recent move out of the hardware business into multiplatform operating environments), and the object-oriented operating system from Taligent (another Apple-IBM joint venture) also provide opportunities for you to stand out from others. If, say, an organization is making a major commitment to Windows NT, any experience you have early in that operating environment's product life cycle may give you the edge in job competitions. Combining this example with a new hardware environment, consider the combination of Digital Equipment Alpha-based systems running Windows NT. Experience with such a system could give you a huge advantage in seeking employment with an organization going in that direction in its desktop computing environment.

5.4 Mobile Computing

Many of you have seen mobile computing devices of the type used by delivery services such as United Parcel Service to record delivery information or hand-held supermarket inventory management systems. Though not by nature "desktop" computing devices, mobile computing nevertheless shares much with personal computers in terms of operating on different paradigms from the more traditional mainframe and minicomputer systems. Specialized input and output, different applications development techniques, and widespread usage of advanced technologies characterize mobile computing as leading-edge with respect to where information systems are headed.

As such, there is not a great deal of expertise with mobile computing technology among people in the job market. For example, the database and transaction management models for such devices must be very different from those of "regular" computer systems. The location of a mobile device when it requests a data management or transaction operation is not predictable, and query optimization algorithms, network routing, and other services must take this uncertainty into account. More importantly for our discussion in this book, developers of mobile computing applications must understand these distinctions and be able to (1) communicate that understanding during interviews and (2) act on that knowledge as they implement mobile computing systems. Experience in this area will be highly advantageous for years to come, given the growing reliance on mobile computing and the lack of widespread experience with such technology.

5.5   Systems Integration

Downsizing (the technology trend which has driven our discussion about moving your skills base to desktop technology) and heterogeneity have proved to be a troublesome combination for most organizations over the past decade. Conceptually, the principle behind moving to distributed smaller-scale systems is a straightforward one: If you take some number of smaller devices, network them together, and have applications that communicate among the various systems, then even if you have products from different vendors, the combination of standards and gateways will enable you to hook your components together with relative ease.

As anyone who has ever done any systems integration will confirm, though, the process is anything but easy. Even though communications and networking technology have matured to the point where basic connectivity is easy to attain, *interoperability* among small-scale systems over any type of environment, whether departmental or enterprise-wide, is still extremely difficult to accomplish.

Even with the downsizing trend, many organizations still retain some degree of mainframe and/or minicomputer presence in their information systems environments. Application front-ends may move to the desktop, but very often the "guts" of application processing, or large-scale services such as managing very large databases, remains within the domain of the data center and large computer systems.

This presents a tremendous opportunity for mainframe and minicomputer programmers who are moving their skills to the desktop. Keep in mind that many of today's colleges and universities have shifted the focus of their computer science and information systems programs to personal computers, rather than timesharing on main-frames or midrange systems. Therefore, many of the most qualified PC-literate computer professionals have little or no experience with the systems that you do, such as IBM mainframes or Digital Equipment VAX minicomputers. Systems integration means just what the term says: *integrating* diverse types of computer systems to make them work together. Because of this, a broad skills base *that includes mainframe or minicomputer skills* is often useful in acquiring a position of this type.

Further, the need for systems integration skills will only increase over the next few years, as the last holdouts from any form of desktop computing find themselves at least bringing PCs and workstations into their fold. Therefore, keep your eyes peeled for opportunities in which the marriage of *both* your newly learned skills and those of your previous life can serve you well.

5.6 Systems Migration and Transition

Another area in which skills both on large systems and in desktop environments are useful is in migrating and moving applications and systems. As organizations struggle with implementing client/server computing (discussed in a moment), portions of applications—if not entire applications themselves—are moved from large systems to PCs and workstations. To successfully accomplish this migration, particularly with partial applications, it's desirable to have some knowledge of the programming language, operating system, and other environmental factors of the source environment as well as their counterparts in the target environment. As we discussed with respect to systems integration, your past large systems experience can give you an edge for this type of position over a competitor who has worked exclusively with desktop systems.

5.7 Groupware

In desktop computing environments, particularly those based on PCs, the ability for workgroups—collections of people working on similar tasks together—to function in an automated manner has been spotty, at best. Even with high-quality LAN connectivity, the type of collaboration found on larger systems, particularly ones like DEC VAX minicomputers, has been lacking until recently.

As an example, consider the Digital Equipment product VAXNotes, an electronic conferencing system. Users on a DEC network (typically DECNet) can sign on to different types of VAXNotes subject-oriented conferences and, under various topics, enter base notes and replies. Basically functioning as bulletin boards, the conferences provide a logically centralized repository for project-related communications (as well as other-than-work subjects, such as sports or hobbies).

In the PC world, the only equivalent until recently was dialing up remote bulletin boards, often on distant mainframe or minicomputer systems, and functioning as a terminal in much the same way as the above VAXNotes usage model. With the introduction of products such as Lotus Notes and Microsoft Windows for Workgroups, the PC world now has a high degree of groupware capability in which you could specialize, giving yourself an advantage over the more traditional type of PC-oriented computer professional.

5.8 Workflow

Somewhat related to groupware, workflow systems enable systems designers to specify the flow of work among a department or, in larger cases, across an enterprise in an automated manner. Work might be the routing that an insurance document must take for approval, or the flow of a systems design document among PC developers and their supervisors and managers. Workflow, like groupware, is somewhat more complex to implement in distributed PC environments than in centralized mainframe or minicomputer systems, so here is another specialty area through which you can differentiate yourself.

5.9 Client/Server Computing

Client/server computing—the cure-all for everything from application development bottlenecks to lack of world peace. Arguably the most hyped technological concept of the past decade (closely followed by open systems and object-oriented computing), client/server computing is much like systems integration, which we discussed earlier: It's conceptually very simple, yet implementation can be extremely tricky and complex.

Whether your desktop computing specialty is oriented towards PCs or workstations, you undoubtedly will find yourself involved with client/server computing—at least if you hope to continue to advance through the balance of your career. Whether you're writing service routines for servers, callable from standards-based application programming interfaces (APIs), or writing client applications designed to interface with back-end servers, the days of monolithic, centralized applications are fading away (at least among newly developed applications—the large COBOL/VSAM/IMS/CICS programs that run most of corporate America and government agencies will remain alive; hence the need for systems integration, as we discussed earlier).

As we'll note in Chap. 8, the topic of client/server computing can be a boon to your job search if you have gained experience via your self-training program (or through other means). However, the topic can also be a pitfall, as when you are asked about client/server technology, it's easy to slip into marketing-ese and make statements about dramatic cost savings over mainframe systems (mostly unproven, at least on a large scale), ease of development and maintenance (somewhat true), and the effortless way in which clients and servers are plugged into one another to magically form systems (it doesn't work that way). Be careful to avoid the hype, as we'll discuss, and focus on technology and facts, and you can stand apart from others when competing for the many client/server positions available.

5.10   Rapid Prototyping

As we noted earlier in this book, the systems development paradigm for desktop systems is often weighted towards rapid prototyping methodologies (i.e., quick development without a lot of overhead and formality) rather than long-drawn-out developmental life cycles. By gaining familiarity with a number of rapid prototyping tools—CASE-based code generators, screen and forms managers, advanced 4GLs, etc.—you can effectively compete for positions with companies and organizations that demand quick turnaround without the prolonged, meeting-driven approach that usually characterizes mainframe and minicomputer development efforts.

5.11   GUI Development

It is highly desirable that GUI development be part of your repertoire, along with database programming, networking and communications, and other areas, and there is still a demand (and will be for some time) for development efforts focusing primarily on GUIs. For example, one of the tasks related to client/server computing (discussed above) might be to take an existing mainframe legacy application and redevelop it in a client/server mold using a 3GL such as C and a native GUI system such as Motif or Open Look. In the absence of rapid development tools, the client software must be developed in such a way that a GUI environment can be created; this means a certain application architecture (event-driven software), management of system resource files in which menu and other information is maintained, and so on.

In environments such as this, your GUI development skills can outweigh any deficiencies in your skill set (such as lack of PC database experience). Be careful, though, not to become too specialized and locked into GUI development, given the multifunctional nature of most desktop computing positions.

5.12 Chapter Summary

In this chapter, we've taken a brief look at a number of different specialties through which you can help differentiate yourself from the pack once you have successfully made the transition to desktop computing environments. Additionally, you can use this list, as well as updates you make yourself *as you constantly stay up to date with emerging technologies* (hint, hint), to guide your training program as you get set to make the jump into PCs and workstations. For example, you should absolutely get some level of client/server computing experience; by following the advice in Chap. 4 and purchasing not one but two personal computers (or having two available for your use), you can teach yourself to write client/server applications using whatever tools and facilities you feel are most pertinent to your future prospects.

6

Interim Consulting

6.1 Introduction

For many of you, your transition into desktop computing will occur
through consulting, or some other form of nonpermanent, contractual
employment. Whether you choose to stay with a consulting role,
building your own practice based on your PC, LAN, and other newly
acquired skills, or eventually move back into a corporate setting,
interim consulting experience can be a valuable addition to your general career repertoire.

In this chapter, we'll focus on the areas which will help you define
your consulting-related goals, identify target opportunities, hone your
skills to meet those opportunities, and sell yourself through your
technical merits and interpersonal skills, the purpose being to lock in
desktop computing consulting projects.

6.2 Defining Your Consulting Goals

In Chap. 2, I related how I first became involved with computer consulting, my primary goal being to provide myself with a channel for
learning as much as I could about PC technology and to supplement
my mainframe software development experience. Before you embark
on any consulting activities, it's important to focus on why you are
doing so.

6.2.1 Preemptive part-time consulting

Some of you may still be working in a mainframe or minicomputer
environment, but either awaiting an imminent career disruption (lay-

off, voluntary severance, etc.) or facing the realities of a derailed career path. Basically, you have yet to be downsized, but it's probably a matter of time, and even if it doesn't occur, your career climb is likely to be permanently over.

In such a case, you may have already made up your mind that it's time to retrain yourself and build a skills base oriented toward desktop computing. In addition to the self-training program you have undertaken (discussed in Chap. 4), an excellent "final exam" of your acquired knowledge is to put it to use in a part-time consulting setting.

For example, if you spend several months teaching yourself a PC database program like FoxPro, Paradox, or Microsoft Access, you could develop a small-scale departmental or small business system to do inventory management, sales order control, or some other function. With *demonstrated* success in your newly acquired skills, full-time employment—or further consulting assignments—in desktop computing areas will be even easier to attain.

6.2.2   A trial run at a change of scenery

Perhaps you have already been forced into undertaking the technological transition we've been discussing in this book, but you're uncertain if you really want to get back into corporate life. Perhaps the events that led up to your career transition have left you with somewhat of a distaste for being a corporate employee, with a great deal of your career and personal future controlled by others. Maybe you envision similar difficulties befalling you in the future as some other type of technological paradigm shift occurs.

Having been an employee for your entire career, though, you are uncertain and somewhat wary about your prospects in the consulting and contract work world. As we'll discuss shortly, your technical skills, no matter how up to date, are only one part of the overall picture that makes you a successful consultant. Can you market your services? Can you manage a consulting practice—track and predict cash flow, find and successfully work with subcontractors or employees, and plan for the future of your business?

The nice thing about consulting, particularly when you orient your efforts toward PCs, LANs, and desktop computing, is that you can embark on a trial run, whether for a short period of time (e.g., several months) or for some longer duration. You may find that you not only enjoy working with desktop computing technology but enjoy working on your own, controlling your own destiny (as much as possible) rather than being subordinated to corporate goals established at far-away headquarters. Conversely, the uncertainty of consulting and contract work may not be conducive to your particular mindset; you may find that you are extremely anxious when you are between projects, and would prefer the comfort of a steady paycheck.

Regardless of where your long-term path will take you, the opportunity to try consulting on an interim basis as part of your technological transition can be very valuable to you. Even if you do eventually decide to head back into corporate life, the experience gained (just as with part-time, moonlighting consulting, as discussed in the previous section) will greatly aid you in achieving full-time employment using desktop computing systems.

6.2.3   A permanent career change

Finally, in the context of our discussion in the previous sections, you may indeed find that the flexibility, control, and other aspects of consulting are very much to your liking, and your career and technical focus will indeed shift to new directions at the same time. As we'll discuss later in this chapter, one of the attractive things about consulting in general, and PC-oriented consulting in particular, is that you have tremendous opportunities to continually do something new, sometimes building on your previous experience (e.g., going from dBASE III+ programming to FoxPro for Windows development) and in other cases moving to different areas (e.g., moving from stand-alone software development to Novell NetWare systems installations, configurations, and management for clients). The breadth of skills you acquire from your work is likely to be much wider than in corporate environments, even those that feature PCs, workstations, and LANs. Consider that many corporate environments impose desktop computing standards upon their departmental organizations, perhaps requiring that each and every departmental LAN be configured as follows:

- Novell NetWare as the network operating system
- 386 or 486 PCs only
- FoxPro for Windows as the only database product
- Microsoft Excel as the only spreadsheet manager
- WordPerfect for Windows as the only word processor

And so on. If you were to find yourself working in an environment such as this one, your skills base would probably be focused exclusively on the products mentioned above.

In contrast, consulting activities may lead you into the above environment for some period of time, then into another company which uses Banyan Vines networks, Quattro Pro spreadsheets, Microsoft Access database systems, and other products, and then into still other companies using different products and technologies. While your expertise in any of these areas will probably be determined by how long you work with the various products, spending some amount of time with all of the products mentioned above, as well as others, will no doubt provide you with a skills base that will broaden your opportunities with future clients.

6.3   Starting a Consulting Practice

It's not enough to tell yourself (or others) that you are going to do PC consulting or contract work; the process of actually getting started must be understood and put into practice before you can really get going. In this section, we'll briefly discuss the many things you must do, on the business side (e.g., setting up a business and all of the support functions necessary) as well as the technical preparation functions. For more detailed discussions of each of these areas, see *How to Be a Successful Computer Consultant.*[1]

6.3.1   Determining your service offerings

As we've noted throughout this book, there are several aspects to the question, "What will I do in the desktop computing arena?" At one end of the spectrum, your skills base is likely to be broader than that in your mainframe or minicomputer career, encompassing software development, LAN management, systems management, and other disciplines. At the other end, though, you need to have some idea of the specific technologies and products with which you'll work. This is *especially* true in the PC consulting world, even more than in corporate settings.

Consider the reasons that companies and organizations hire consultants and contract assistance. Chief among them is lack of in-house expertise with products and/or technologies that are, for one reason or another, important to the future systems development efforts of that organization. Therefore, a hiring manager looking for a PC database development consultant will probably want experience in the product(s) in use at that company, or at least want to be convinced that

---

[1]A. Simon, *How to Be a Successful Computer Consultant,* 3d ed., McGraw-Hill, New York, 1994.

you can quickly build on your expertise with similar products and be able to satisfy his or her development requirements (for example, if you know FoxPro Version 2.5 for DOS and the organization uses FoxPro Version 2.5 for Windows, your skills base in the former product is easily transferable to the latter product, and you should be able to convince the hiring authority of this).

Given our discussion above, this means that you should do one of the following:

- Build on the desktop computing skills base that you already have, either from previous corporate experience or from your self-training program (discussed in Chap. 4).

- Direct your self-training program (again, discussed in Chap. 4) toward those products and technologies that you believe will be most beneficial to your prospective consulting activities.

Particularly for the latter of these two choices, *market research* is important. By market research, I don't necessarily mean any type of formal survey, hanging out at shopping malls with a clipboard and asking passersby about what types of PC products they think are most important to their businesses. Rather, your research efforts should include the following:

- Scanning the classified and display advertisements for both consulting and full-time employment, particularly in major cities. The Sunday edition of *The New York Times,* for instance, contains literally hundreds of advertisements each week, both from actual companies looking for consultants and contract workers (as well as full-time employees) and from consulting-oriented headhunters (commonly known as brokers). While a large percentage of the brokers are simply trying to build up their résumé database, and don't really have "current, *immediate,* high-paying openings for CA-Clipper, MS Access, FoxPro, SQL Server, Oracle…[continue the list with another dozen DBMS products]," these lists are valuable to *you* in that you can see what products these folks think are most likely to lead to their placing consultants with client companies. For example, if you notice a tremendous increase in requests for Microsoft Access skills among the various advertisements, it wouldn't be erroneous to assume that there indeed might be an increase in requests for developers skilled in that product, and therefore time spent learning Microsoft Access would not be time wasted.

- Reading trade magazines, business periodicals, and other sources, the goal being to determine what "really hot" products are coming to market or, in a broader sense, what technologies are likely to be important. For example, if you see that a major vendor such as Lotus or Microsoft is bringing to market some highly touted product that promises "new breakthroughs in open client/server object-oriented development," and if that product indeed receives excellent reviews in *PC Magazine, Byte,* and other computer periodicals and is even discussed in business magazines such as *Business Week* or *Forbes,* it is likely that there will be a near-term demand for consultants with experience in that particular product. Therefore, building expertise with that product into your consulting service offerings may assist you in gaining contract work.

- Looking for highly saturated areas in which many consultants have staked a claim. If you already have spent time in such an area, some diversification and broadening of your own offerings is in order *right now.* If you haven't been in that area, perhaps it is one that is best avoided because of the overcrowding.

- And finally, asking good old-fashioned questions of either individuals who are likely to be consulting clients or those with whom some type of business relationship may be formed. We'll discuss strategic relationships in a moment, but asking a dozen or so consulting services brokers a straightforward question like "What products and technologies are most important to your customers and clients?" should give you a pretty good idea of where to concentrate your efforts.

As was briefly noted above, it is extremely important to have contingency plans in place, particularly in the PC marketplace. I noted in *How to Be a Successful Computer Consultant* that back in the early 1980s, my original service offerings were going to be oriented around PC software product training (word processing, spreadsheets, etc.), as my own market research indicated a tremendously growing market for those types of services. However, once the local computer stores started offering such classes, mostly as loss leaders (e.g., charging a nominal amount or nothing at all for hands-on training, the purpose being to draw potential customers for computer purchases into the store), I quickly shifted my own efforts toward database application development. Without those contingency plans in place, my efforts might well have faltered at that point.

6.3.2 Strategic relationships

In the previous section, we briefly discussed the concept of building strategic relationships with those likely to be able to provide you with

PC consulting opportunities. When I first began consulting, my initial projects were done in conjunction with a local computer retailer; I would develop custom database applications for customers who had purchased hardware systems from the store.

Even though the PC retailing market has changed dramatically, moving away from local, independently owned retailers and even national showroomlike chains to warehouselike superstores and a substantial mail-order contingent, you can still contact the technical support manager or another executive at a local computer superstore, provide your business marketing literature, and offer to contractually do custom software development or perform other consulting functions for any customers who desire such services. Though some of these stores may have their own in-house staff to do this type of work, there is always the possibility that (1) their staff is overworked and cannot fill a particular opportunity or (2) you have some expertise that they currently lack (perhaps their only Paradox for Windows developer left the company, and they have yet to find a full-time replacement when an opportunity occurs).

On a broader scope, there are the consulting services brokers discussed earlier in this chapter, although, as I related in *How to Be a Successful Computer Consultant,*[2] receiving an opportunity from this channel is basically a crapshoot. You're often competing against the "house favorites" (consultants who have been used for a long period of time and who are placed steadily with the broker's clients) for any given position, and gauging real opportunities from the volumes listed in the Sunday classifieds or on bulletin boards is extremely difficult—many either don't exist, are of the form "we *might* need some help next month in Paradox; I'll let you know, but in the meantime, could you send us some résumés?" (this being the conversation between the end client and the broker), or for whatever other reason don't really materialize.

Therefore, it is important—*especially* if you have left your full-time employment (voluntarily or not) and are trying to use consulting as a means of making the transition into the desktop computing world—not to rely on any one channel in the area of strategic relationships. Some may work well, others may not, so explore any and all alternatives.

6.3.3   Starting a business

Even if your motives for pursuing consulting are defensive in nature (preemptively cushioning yourself against an impending layoff) or

---

[2]Ibid., pp. 75–81.

only transitory (e.g., providing a way to "earn while you learn," that is, supplementing your self-training program for desktop computing skills with some temporary on-the-job training), you still need to approach consulting as a business practice. Organizing a business, managing its finances, finding and keeping clients, filing all of the correct business and tax forms in a timely manner—all of these items need to be as much a part of your consulting efforts (again, even if you are only doing this on a trial or transitory basis) as the technical services you offer and the areas in which you specialize.

Let's take a brief look at each of these subjects.

Organizing a consulting business.   Some of the things you need to consider are discussed below.

- *Your form of business organization.*   You can remain what is known as a *sole practitioner* (basically, someone in business for himself or herself, with no other legal structure to his or her business), although in recent years tax laws and Internal Revenue Service (IRS) rulings have dramatically limited this option for most individuals. In short, there is a list of 20 items which help determine whether or not you are in fact an employee of an organization, regardless of whether you and that organization choose to term you as such. Basically, if you work at an organization's site, using its materials (e.g., computers, software), and if you are at that location on a regular basis (particularly if the organization dictates your hours to you), you are considered an employee of that company. If you are working for a broker or another "middleman" at a client's site, you may be considered an employee of the broker company. Alternatively, you may *incorporate* as a business; in this case you can contract with any other company and be assured of retaining independent contractor status. The tradeoffs between these two types of organization (a third type is a *partnership,* which obviously implies having at least one partner in your efforts) are numerous, including legal protection (a corporation offers an additional layer of protection between you and the rest of the world), benefits (as an employee, you are entitled to some level of benefits, which varies from state to state and which may well vary in the years ahead as a result of national health care reorganization), and deductibility of expenses (as an employee, your travel to a "job" is considered commuting, which is not deductible; as a party in a corporation, your business expenses, including daily or other types of travel, are usually deductible, subject to any changes in the tax laws—the deductibility of meals, for example, keeps changing with time and tax law modifications).

- *Where you will work.* Particularly if you are pursuing consulting on an interim or trial basis, you should plan on working from your home rather than leasing any type of office space. This is especially true if you are doing most or all of your work at a client's site; control of expenses is critical for any consultant, whether full-time or part-time, and there is little reason to spend money on seldom used office space. Particularly today, it is perfectly acceptable and understandable to work from your home; there is little prestige in being "a real consultant with an office," and in fact by avoiding those unnecessary expenses you can lower your fees accordingly, something your clients will appreciate.

- *Supplies and materials.* Business cards, letterhead and envelopes, a computer and software (which you should already have as part of your self-training program)—these are some of the supplies and materials that you will need as you begin your consulting efforts. As with office space, you should endeavor to keep your expenses to a reasonable amount.

- *A business name.* You may choose to do business under your own name (e.g., Ralph Balkan Consulting Services or simply Ralph Balkan, Consultant) or choose a descriptive name such as Desktop Technology Services or InfoServe. Be careful not to make your name *too* restrictive, so that prospective clients bypass you because they believe you not to be appropriate for their business. If, for example, you call your firm John Wilson Desktop Medical Systems, you are specifically targeting hospitals, doctors' offices, and similar markets...but excluding law offices, accounting firms, small businesses, and other potential clients. Perhaps this is intentional; you may want to work only with medical clients, and many consultants operate this way. In the context of our discussion in this book, however—doing PC-related consulting *specifically* to aid your personal technology transition effort—you probably don't want to eliminate prospective clients.

- *Services (and possibly products).* Earlier in this chapter, we discussed the service offerings you might provide, in terms of specific products and technologies. You may wish to focus your efforts exclusively on a small subset of products (e.g., Visual Basic and Paradox for Windows development, exclusively). Alternatively, you may broaden your horizons to be not just a contractual, point product worker but rather a provider of desktop information systems solutions. When you consider that even in the PC world, the development platform (specifically, the software system or language) is dependent on what type of system you are developing, it is arguable that different clients' systems would require different developmental techniques and products. One client's system might best be developed in the C programming language because of low-level systems interaction, while another might be more appropriately generated from a PC-based CASE environment using a code generator. You need to ensure that you don't spread yourself too thin among these types of technologies, but by providing information systems solutions rather than contract product-specific "body shop" work, you can broaden your future base of opportunities, whether in the consulting arena or after you return to the corporate world.

- *Advertising.* For the most part, you can avoid any type of expensive advertising. You may want to place an advertisement in one or more Yellow Pages volumes in the geographic areas you wish to target, and you might want to draw up fliers or brochures for distribution to potential strategic partners (computer retailers, headhunters, etc.). You should avoid newspaper advertising in the interest of cash conservation, and certainly radio and television advertising should be avoided.

Managing finances.   While running your business, even on a part-time basis, you need to manage the firm's finances in a professional, businesslike manner. This includes

- *Separation of funds.*   It's not a good idea to intermingle your business and personal funds, even if you are working as a sole practitioner and on a part-time or interim basis. At the very least, you should keep accurate records of all revenues and expenditures, particularly those that involve use of a home-based office (the rules change every couple of years, usually getting more restrictive) and the business use of a vehicle. Ideally, you should maintain a separate business checking account, depositing all revenues into that account and paying all expenses from that account.

- *Budgeting and cash flow management.*   It's especially important to those of you who are using consulting as your exclusive source of revenue (e.g., you aren't moonlighting while still holding a full-time job) to be able to predict the cash flow from your consulting operations, both in the revenue and expenditure sides. Figure 6.1 illustrates a sample cash flow analysis. While subject to change, of course, having some idea of not only how much you are taking in and spending but also *when* those cash transfers will occur will help you anticipate potential shortfalls (e.g., having to dip into personal funds or quickly finding alternative employment).

Cash Budget
Jordan Business Computer Systems

	JANUARY	FEBRUARY	MARCH	APRIL
Projected revenue				
collections	3000.00	500.00	1000.00	500.00
1st month (70%)	2100.00	350.00	700.00	350.00
2nd month (30%)		900.00	150.00	300.00
Total	2100.00	1250.00	850.00	650.00
Receipts				
Total collections	2100.00	1250.00	850.00	650.00
Bank loan	1000.00			
Total	3100.00	1250.00	850.00	650.00
Payments				
Letterhead	75.00			
Business cards	25.00			
Post office box	15.00			
Accounting services		50.00		
Answering machine	150.00			
Office supplies	25.00	10.00	5.00	7.50
Phone (business)	10.00	10.00	10.00	10.00
Yellow Pages ad		12.50	12.50	12.50
Miscellaneous				
advertising			75.00	60.00
Total	300.00	82.50	102.50	90.00
Beginning cash balance	—	2800.00	3967.50	4715.00
Net cash gain loss for				
current month	2800.00	1167.50	747.50	560.00
Ending cash balance	2800.00	3967.50	4715.00	5275.00

Figure 6.1 Sample estimated cash flow analysis.

- *Billing.* You need to bill your clients in a timely manner, the purpose being to ensure that you receive critically needed payments in time for any business cash outlays you will have. Similarly, you should pay all expenditures in a timely manner, to keep your business reputation intact.

- *Financial statements.* You will have to file federal and state tax returns, very likely quarterly estimated payments, 1099 forms for subcontractor payments, payroll tax withholding forms for any employees you have, and many other types of forms. You need to make sure that you are aware of all filing requirements you have on behalf of your business, and to file those forms (or formal requests for extensions, which are other forms) before any deadlines.

Finding and keeping clients.   Earlier in this chapter, we discussed means by which you can find your initial consulting clients. Once you have become established, you can often rely on word of mouth from *satisfied* clients (don't underestimate the emphasis on "satisfied," as dissatisfied clients are certainly no means on which to build a business practice) to others, whether outside your control (e.g., a client tells a business associate what a wonderful FoxPro applications developer you are) or by using a client as a reference for prospective customers that you find yourself.

You should also not underestimate the power of repeat business and its potential to sustain your consulting activities if you so choose. One trick is to always propose enhancements and additions to systems you develop as part of a prospective follow-on contract. In addition, many satisfied clients will return to you repeatedly for modifications and upgrades, providing you with new work. For example, a client for whom you develop a stand-alone PC-based system may choose to upgrade to a multiuser, LAN-based environment. If the client is pleased with your work, you are likely to get that project (and gain additional experience in technologies with which you may not already be familiar, an added bonus in the context of our discussion in this book).

Legal considerations.   There are a number of legal issues which you must be aware of in the context of your consulting. First, there are different types of filing requirements—which also vary from one geographical area to another—for the type of business organization you choose. Sole proprietors should register their business names with local county clerks or other officials, ensuring that (1) they aren't encroaching on anyone else's business name and (2) no one else can legally use the name they register. Those forming a business as a corporation also need to register their business name, typically with the state corporate commission in conjunction with their legal business filings.

All client work should be done under some type of contract, one which clearly specifies what is expected of you and in what time frame, how much money you are to receive, when you are to receive it and what conditions trigger payments (e.g., monthly payments, passed on deliverables, etc.), and all other aspects of the business relationship between you and all other appropriate parties.

6.4   Conflicts of Interest and Relationships with Your Former Company

Considering the context of our discussion in this chapter—consulting as part of your personal technology transition effort, rather than consulting for the sake of the discipline—there is a good chance that you will be consulting on a moonlighting basis, in parallel with (the last days of?) your full-time employment. You need to ensure that you are aware of any contractual obligations you have to your employer with respect to conflicts of interest; such terms should be clearly spelled out in any employment contract or agreement you have.

For the most part, if you are in the process of being laid off, you should have a great deal of leeway to go after PC-oriented consulting work even with clients of your soon-to-be-former company; in fact, you may even find your employer more willing to work with you on such a project (e.g., to subcontract work to you) as you are leaving the company (or after you have left) than when you were "an employee in good standing." Stereotypes and restrictive views often break down when the relationship between an employee and a former company changes, and the manager who was unwilling to give you a chance to do desktop computing work when you were employed there might very well be willing to work with you once you have set up shop on your own, particularly if you have a demonstrated record of success with other clients or can prove that your self-training program has made you well qualified for the task at hand. It seems strange, but then again, so is most of what you are probably going through as you endure such an abrupt career transition.

The main point, though, is to be very aware of any obligations you have to your current or former employer with respect to conflicts of interest and to abide by them. It will be extremely difficult to build up some type of postemployment business relationship if you have a dispute with the firm regarding such matters.

6.5   Business Plan

It is important to all consultants, even transitory or temporary ones, to have a written business plan in which all of the subjects discussed in this chapter plus many others (competition, financial projections, staffing plans, etc.) are detailed. If you are simply in the business to make a technology transition, you can probably avoid a lengthy business plan of the type you would submit when seeking a bank loan or outside investment. At the very least, though, you should have a four- to six-page document in which your plans are *written*. You can then subsequently refer to the document throughout your practice (updating it as necessary), as well as perform a sanity check on your plans (which is far easier to do when reviewing a written document than when mentally going through numerous items).[3]

6.6   Interviewing for Consulting Positions

In Part 2 of this book, we present a number of sample interview questions of the type you are likely to face during your job search. For the most part, interviews for consulting positions are likely to include many of the same types of questions, with one very important difference: A prospective client cares very little about your career aspirations and personal objectives (e.g., the questions in Chap. 8), and with very few exceptions you won't be asked questions like "Where do you see yourself in 3 to 5 years?" Consulting-oriented interviews will primarily focus on how well you know the product(s) in use at the firm that is considering your services, or in cases where you are being considered for general development services (e.g., no predetermined products but rather such choices are left to your discretion), you will be asked questions about your development philosophy and experience.

Of course, if you are interviewing for a full-time consulting position with an employer who provides consulting services, you will be asked the types of questions presented in Chap. 8, but that is primarily because you are seeking full-time employment (or at least long-term contract consulting work). In cases where you are being considered primarily because of your technical abilities for some temporary period, your interviews will focus on technologies and products, so be prepared.

6.7   Chapter Summary

Obviously, a single short chapter can't tell you everything you need to know about computer consulting, but that isn't our purpose here. Rather, it is best recognized that even if you have no desire to work on your own and are simply looking for the most expedient way back into corporate life—involved with desktop computing technologies rather than whatever environment you find yourself being squeezed out of—job searches can be lengthy, particularly because of your technology transition process. Therefore, you may find yourself forced into

---

[3]A sample business plan is presented in ibid., pp. 104–117.

contract work or other types of consulting activities while you continue your job search.

An important consideration is ethics; if you make a commitment (especially a contractual one) to a client for, say, six months of full-time consulting, you are ethically committed to serving that client regardless of what full-time or more lucrative consulting work comes along. It is entirely possible that you could negotiate some sort of shift to part-time work with your client, or a transition to a replacement, but the client is under no obligation to accommodate you. As long as a client is meeting its end of the agreement (providing the appropriate support and resources, and, most importantly, paying you), you should *never* walk out on the client. It's a small world out there, and reputations for untrustworthiness tend to follow you wherever you head.

As we noted earlier, you may very well find yourself enthralled with the consulting life, seeing it as infinitely preferable to the type of corporate atmosphere from which you find yourself being eliminated. Many people, though, have no temperament for the consulting lifestyle, and are more likely to view consulting as a stopping point on their way back into corporate life. Regardless of which category you belong to—or whether you could go in either direction—it's important to recognize consulting and contract work as part of your transition process into desktop computing technology.

7

Lifestyle Adjustment

7.1 Introduction

In this short chapter, we will discuss corollary aspects of your technology transition effort and job search. It is unfortunate, but it is very likely that your efforts in these areas are occurring at the same time as other lifestyle disruptions. Based on the point system which ranks major events in one's life (birth of a child, various relatives' deaths, relocation, job change, marriage, divorce, etc.) and assigns risk factors to each event, you are probably treading in dangerous territory. For example, if you were laid off from your previous job and are still unemployed, the process of not only looking for a job but trying to retrain yourself in more marketable skills than those which you currently possess will increase the pressure on you. Add in factors such as potential relocation because of a new job, family pressures (e.g., when you find a new job, there may be extensive travel required even if you don't have to relocate), financial concerns, and other items, and you should have an idea of the stress that you are under.

We'll briefly run down several of these items, our focus being to try to keep each of the areas in context and not to permit any one area (or a combination of several) to cause you serious problems.

7.2 Relocation

Perhaps you have no strong feelings one way or another about the possibility of relocating to some other part of the country, whether close to where you currently live or further away. You may be renting an apartment, have few ties to family and friends in the area, not have children in schools...in short, your tenure in your current geographical location may be transitory.

It could be, though, that you are very closely tied to your communi-ty. Perhaps it's your hometown, or a place where you longed to live until you finally achieved that goal. You may have children in school, and most of us who moved to another city as a child are aware of the trauma and disruption, even if the move is eagerly anticipated. Maybe your spouse or significant other has ties to the area (family, a job of his or her own, etc.) and is absolutely against any type of reloca-tion.

For the most part, you can safely concentrate your job search in your local community or one within commuting distance. It is well worth being aware, though, of the phenomenon of regional recessions that began in the early 1980s and has continued in earnest.[1] Most importantly, you need to be aware of the effects of being stuck in a region that is currently deep in recession (or at least stagnation) and in which job prospects are somewhat limited. At the time this is being written, the northeastern United States is just now pulling out of a three-year slowdown after a long period of above-average growth and economic health, although most of the rest of the United States had long since begun recovering in earnest. California, however, is still mired in recession, particularly southern California, the area which had had one the longest periods of sustained growth.

The point is that while there will always be some prospective employment opportunities (during the Great Depression the unem-ployment rate topped out at 25 percent, which meant that 75 percent of the people in the country still had jobs), your prospects will be somewhat limited if you are unwilling to consider transferring to another geographical area. Note that there is nothing wrong with this (for example, I had personal reasons for remaining in Colorado for a number of years while the economy was far less robust there than in other areas); you should just understand the ramifications of deci-sions such as this one.

7.3 Personal Finances

If you are currently unemployed or facing unemployment, you should be *very* careful in managing your personal finances until you find a new position. It's very tempting to take a large portion of a lump-sum severance payment that you may have received and spend it on per-sonal goods (such as a new car), but you should *immediately* enter cash conservation mode until your financial position becomes clearer.

---

[1]Discussed in both A. Simon, *The Computer Professional's Survival Guide,* McGraw-Hill, New York, 1992, pp. 3–5, and A. Simon, *How to Be a Successful Computer Consultant,* 3d ed., McGraw-Hill, New York, 1994, p. 29.

There are numerous books which discuss managing your personal finances, and you should understand all of the options available to you with respect to asset and debt management and other areas.

7.4 Your Mind-Set

If you were involuntarily terminated from your previous employment—laid off, in lay terms—you wouldn't be human if it didn't bother you at least a little. Even if you were getting totally fed up with your former company and were almost looking forward to some type of opportunity to move your career in a new direction, it hurts to think that you weren't considered valuable enough for that company to retain as it moves in new directions.

Forget it; it's over! The past is the past, and there is no use reliving career choices you either made or didn't make, wondering how things might have been different if you had taken different paths at various points some number of years ago. Further, you shouldn't take it personally. I once interviewed someone who had been part of a mass layoff at a Philadelphia-area software company, who related that the downsizings there had been part of the CEO's desire to make the staff as lean as possible and still meet business requirements. There was no major business crisis, the company was not losing money—it was just "the thing to do" to disrupt a large number of peoples' lives. In fact, it has almost become trendy for CEOs to participate in the downsizing trend, even when it really isn't necessary.

CEO 1: "I announced 5000 job cuts."

CEO 2: "Oh yeah? Well, I just announced 10,000 layoffs!"

CEO 3: "That's nothing! I'm going to cut 20,000 people and I'm going to do it in *this* fiscal year, not over two or three years like you wimps!"

The above might sound rather cynical, but don't underestimate the pressure CEOs are under from boards of directors to produce results. A large number of CEOs have found themselves evicted from the executive suite in the past couple of years, including one person who was forced out ostensibly because he wouldn't make job cuts that he felt could be postponed or not executed at all.

The point is that unlike in times past, being forcibly terminated from a job is arguably no reflection on *you,* but rather an indication that you simply were in the wrong place at the wrong time. Regardless of how long your job search takes, *don't* mope around the house, *don't* consider yourself to be worthless, *don't* let any discouragement seep over into your personal relationships. Rather, take the approach that was espoused by the singing Mother Superior of "Climb Every Mountain" fame in *The Sound of Music*. Regardless of what your religious convictions are (or even if you have any), the following philosophy should be kept in mind whenever possible:

When God closes a door, He opens another.

Simply put, even the most discouraging turn of events often turns out to be a blessing in disguise, depending on how *you* react to the situation and the effort you make to meet the challenges that await you. Oftentimes, something like a layoff gives you a bit of a kick in the butt, getting you out of complacency mode and into the realization that your future is often dependent on your own personal efforts (together with a good deal of luck, of course). Give it your best!

7.5 Chapter Summary

In the previous chapters we've discussed topics like conducting an honest self-assessment of your own personal strengths on which you can build, as well as the mechanics of résumé preparation, finding possible employment opportunities, and interviewing. The success of these efforts is often influenced by factors such as your own personal outlook. If you are confident, looking forward to new challenges that await you, this will be reflected in your interviewing processes and *honestly* help give you an edge in job competition. If you have a "weight of the world on your shoulders" attitude, it too will be reflected and interviewers may be hesitant to consider you seriously for employment, no matter how well you have conducted your transition to desktop computing. Keep a positive attitude, understand the parameters of your job search (financial considerations, whether or not you're willing to relocate, etc.), and you are halfway there!

Interviewing

The chapters in this part of the book provide representative questions of the type you are likely to be asked during interviews for PC and desktop computing positions. It's impossible, of course, to include every possible question that you might be asked, and even if it were possible, the purpose of these chapters is not to give you canned answers to such questions that you can parrot back to your interviewer(s).

Rather, these questions, from the general ones in Chap. 8 to the more technology-specific ones in subsequent chapters, are provided to help you get into the mind-set that you'll need for the interviewing process. Along with suggested answers, many of these questions are accompanied by

The questioner's rationale for asking the question; i.e., what is "the question behind the question"

Red flags (answers or partial answers) that you should avoid

Keywords to help you quickly recall the answer when you are asked this question during an interview

In Chap. 3, we briefly discussed interviewing in the context of résumé preparation and the process of locating potential job leads. Before we get into the question-and-answer format of the following chapters, let's briefly discuss some items specific to interviewing for desktop computing positions.

First, it's important to recognize that you inevitably will run into at least one horrible interviewer, someone who (1) asks terrible questions that are totally inapplicable to the position, (2) asks the most obscure, irrelevant technical questions (for example, he or she will ask about C programming skills when the position primarily involves FoxPro development), and / or

(3) has no intention whatsoever of permitting you to "pass" the interview. In these cases, it's recommended that you do the best you possibly can, but be realistic about your chances of securing the position.

Next, understand that no two interviews are the same. In some companies, you will serially interview with several people, one after the other; in other cases, you may find yourself in one or two sessions, with one, two, three, or more interviewers taking turns asking questions—"tag-teaming" you, in a way.

Even in companies that use serial interviewing, the practice will vary from organization to organization. Some interviewing groups meet before they conduct an interview and divide a pool of questions among themselves, hoping to avoid the situation where three or four people ask you the same questions over and over. In other companies, this practice does not exist, and you may very well find yourself answering the question "where do you see yourself in 5 years?" four or five times in the same day.

In serial interviewing, it's important to keep your answers consistent from one interviewer to the next. While it's recommended, of course, that you avoid stretching the truth and especially avoid outright lies which are likely to trip you up, there are less obvious traps that await you. For example, if one interviewer asks the question, "Which do you like better, working alone or in a group?" it's easy to give an off-the-top-of-your-head answer to him or her. Two hours later, in a session with another interviewer, you may be asked the same question. By this second occasion, though, you are dissatisfied with your previous answer; you may have said that you like working alone, but you now modify your answer to be more indicative of adhering to a teamwork philosophy. Inconsistencies in your answers may cause red flags to be raised as you and your abilities are evaluated. "He/she likes to work alone," the first interviewer might say; then another would respond, "That's strange! He/she said that he/she is very teamwork-oriented and likes to work in groups. I wonder which one it is."

Which brings us to our next point: prepare! Whether it's the sample questions from the following pages, other questions you believe are likely to be asked, or company-specific questions (e.g., "What is the working environment like here?"), know your answers and most of the questions you want to ask before you walk into the interview. Of course there will be questions that you have that arise out of the context of the interview, and there no doubt will be unanticipated questions from the interviewers, but you should go into the interview as prepared as possible.

Finally, be confident. Even if this is an interview for your first PC-related job after ten or more years in the mainframe arena, and you have had five such interviews in the past two months and no offers have come from any of them, and even if you were laid off from your previous position as part of one of those wonderful downsizing moves, there is no reason to feel as if you are begging for a position, starting back as an entry-level programmer. With the self-confidence you have gained from your personal training program (Chap. 4) and any formal desktop computing training, plus your accomplishments in the computing field in general regardless of the platform, it is only a matter of time before something positive will come from the interviewing process. Whether you are going for a full-time job or a consulting project, it's important to remember that regardless of the number of false starts and rejections, it takes only one good offer to put you back on track.

8

General
Interview
Questions

In this chapter we'll go through some of the general (i.e., not technology-specific) questions that you are likely to be asked. Most of these questions carry over from interviewing for computer positions in general (not just desktop-related)—or, for that matter, interviewing for any type of job. In our discussion, though, we'll put a desktop computing spin on the answers and behind-the-scenes items.

It's important to note that there is no guarantee that you will be asked any of these questions, although most interviewers go through this type of questioning before they get down to technical specifics. One person whom I interviewed for this book about her interviewing journey for a PC-related position after seven years as a mainframe-oriented requirements analyst in the Air Force told me that during one interview she was immediately bombarded with technical questions concerning some dBASE III+ code she had helped maintain during a moonlighting consulting position. Instead of focusing on her general aptitudes and background, the interviewer went through code listings she had been asked to bring and started picking apart table structures, variable naming conventions, and other factors with which she had nothing whatsoever to do, given that she had only been maintaining code that someone else had written. Needless to say, she wasn't offered a position (and, in the context of our introductory remarks for this part of the book, that experience certainly qualified as a horrible interview with a horrendous interviewer).

In most cases, though, you will find yourself asked many of the following questions, so read on.

Question 1   Why did you leave your last position?

Behind the scenes of the question

If you are no longer employed and are looking for a position, whether in desktop computing in our case or just in general, the interviewer wants to know why you left your position and are currently unemployed. In some cases, you may have been caught in a layoff, either small-scale (e.g., a department of, say, 50 people) or large-scale (maybe several thousand staff members, as entire operations were eliminated). At one time, there was a stigma attached to being laid off, particularly among white-collar professional and technical workers. Given all that has happened in the past five years or so, if you have been laid off, you have plenty of company (well over 100,000 people in the computer profession alone), and there is no "shame" in this fact; it is unlikely that in today's climate anyone will view you as deficient in your abilities or as a failure simply because you were caught up in corporate cost-cutting.

Perhaps, seeing the handwriting on the wall with respect to layoffs, you took a voluntary severance package, or maybe you just resigned because of the lack of career prospects at your former place of employment. Your answer should accurately reflect these facts; don't try to hide anything.

In the case of a voluntary termination on your part, the interviewer is also trying to gauge what the job factors were that caused you to resign. If, say, the problem was a lack of career progression (promotions, compensation, etc.) and the company with which you are interviewing has the same characteristics as your former employer, you probably won't be very happy there and may not last too long. Therefore, the company may not want to bring you aboard, regardless of how well you fit the open position(s) there.

Suggested answer

"I was laid off along with 2500 others, most of them from the support functions at ABC Conglomerates. The data center was heavily affected, with about 400 of the layoffs coming there."

Or

"ABC Conglomerates has been going through 3 years of layoffs, and they offered a voluntary severance package before the next round of layoffs take place early next year. Our department was down about 50 percent in staffing from 3 years ago, and almost certainly the rest of the people are scheduled for job cuts. I figured that this was a good time for me to make a break, take the voluntary severance plan, and get back on track working with more state-of-the-art technology than we had at ABC."

Cautions

As is recommended for interviews of all types, avoid excessive criticism of your former company, your former manager, or former coworkers. It's fine to matter-of-factly point out things like "several years ago, ABC made a commitment to a massive transition program from mainframes to XYZ minicomputers, and by the time the transition had been completed—three years late—the XYZ systems were out of date, maintenance costs were as high as ever, and in general the transition program wasn't very successful." However, you should not give answers like the following (no matter how true they are!):

"My former boss was responsible for setting the strategic technology direction for ABC, and he screwed it up big-time. We totally botched a transition program and got stuck with antiquated minicomputers instead of leapfrogging to PCs and LANs. And then, after messing up the program, he wound up getting promoted, too, leaving the rest of us behind as scapegoats."

Or

"ABC was definitely the worst place I ever worked. They told me that I would get a chance to work with workstations and PCs, and they stuck me doing mainframe COBOL maintenance programming for four years. Every time I tried to get into the newer technologies in other departments, my boss put a halt to my transfer, saying that I was too valuable to release right at the moment...and then they laid me off! What a bunch of $%#@!s they were! Say, you guys aren't like that, are you?"

Question 2   Why are you looking to leave your current position?

Behind the scenes of the question

This question is very similar to the previous one, with the exception that you haven't yet severed your ties with your current employer. Layoffs may be looming, or maybe your career path has stagnated; whatever the reason, the interviewer is trying to gauge your sincerity with respect to terminating your employment if the company were to make you an offer. He or she is trying to make sure you aren't just "fishing," interviewing for the heck of it to see if something good comes up. At the same time (just as with the previous question, in situations where you have already left), the interviewer is trying to gauge why you are seriously considering leaving in order to see if the breakpoint factors are also present at this company and if you will quickly become disenchanted.

Suggested answer

"We're looking at somewhere between 5000 and 10,000 layoffs over the next two years, and I think that my department is likely to be heavily affected by this next round. I would rather take a preemptive approach and find a better career alternative now than wait for that to happen."

Or

"ABC is bringing in junior staff members for most of the PC and workstation projects and leaving the mainframe support staff in place, even though there is a stated corporate goal to move 75 percent of the applications from the mainframe to the desktop within three years. I've spent the past two years training myself to do PC development, and even though on my own time I've developed a number of applications quite similar to those which we use at work, my requests to transfer to the desktop computing group have been repeatedly turned down. Frankly, I see the handwriting on the wall; my job may wind up being eliminated in a couple of years, and I really want to work with PCs and LANs—that's why I've spent so much of my own time training myself in all of these new technologies."

Cautions

Again, avoid personal criticisms of your supervisor or manager, or your current employer as a whole. Be matter-of-fact in assessing shortcomings (see the previous question for an example), but avoid responses like

"I just can't get a promotion at that place. We had a new manager take over two years ago, and she brought her entire staff of managers and supervisors over from DEF Corp., and they have this tight little clique that no one can crack. They all got stock options and all of these perks, and those of us who have been there for ten years and made ABC what it is today got totally screwed over."

(Again, this may be entirely accurate with respect to your situation, but you should avoid the excess negativism.)

Question 3   What are your greatest strengths?

Behind the scenes of the question

This is one of those questions (like the next one, what are your greatest weaknesses?) that are often asked but are, in effect, meaningless. There is little or nothing that you can say here that will tilt a job competition in your favor; if, say, the position is for a Paradox for Windows programmer and you state that your greatest strength is software development using Paradox for Windows, this makes you look rather one-dimensional, with limited capabilities beyond that specific development platform. Even if you are interviewing for a consulting position that specifically requires expertise in Paradox for Windows, stating that your greatest strength is—guess what—development using Paradox for Windows sounds like a forced answer and doesn't exactly ring true.

It's best to stick with a "harmless" answer (actually, several squeezed into one, as you'll see below) emphasizing your problem-solving abilities, quick learning, adaptability, teamwork, and all-around worthiness for sainthood. The answer to this question won't really help you much, so you should just try to ensure that it doesn't hurt you.

Suggested answer

"I'm a very quick learner. Every time I've had to learn a new programming language or software development system, I've always been productive in a matter of days, building on the experience I already had."

(*Note:* The above answer squeezes adaptability, high productivity, and technical competence into a single response.)

Or, if interviewing for a position as a team leader, supervisor, or manager,

"I've always worked extremely well with others, those junior to me as well as peers and senior coworkers. I've been able to help bring junior developers up to speed very quickly, and when functioning as a task leader I've always been able to coordinate my team's work with that of others, resolving problems quickly."

(*Note:* You've tried to establish yourself as a team player, leader, master negotiator, and all-around good guy.)

Question 4 What are your greatest weaknesses?

Behind the scenes of the question

I hate this question! If you have any common sense, you do too! Most of the time, it is asked simply because an interviewer was unimaginative enough to ask you the previous question about your greatest strengths and figures that this corollary question should be asked as well.

No one—I repeat, *no one*—would give an answer to this question that would jeopardize his or her chances of getting the job for which he or she is being interviewed (at least, no one with an ounce of brains). You will *never* hear a reply to this question like "I'm a horrible software developer; my code is totally unreadable, and even though it works, even I can't maintain it." Nor would you ever receive an answer such as "I'm a horrible supervisor; I have no backbone whatsoever, and anyone I've ever managed steamrolls me and totally runs amok, doing whatever he or she feels like doing."

The standard trick to answering this question when it is stupidly asked is to give an answer that in effect plays up your strengths for the position for which you're being interviewed. For example, assume that you are interviewing for a management position in which you would be responsible for three different projects, each led by one of your direct reports. An answer to this question might be something like "I've always been a 'big picture' person, grasping as much as possible about a whole lot of different things. When I get bogged down in excruciating detail, I tend to get impatient." Note that your self-ascribed weakness, impatience with detail, is exactly the attribute that a good multiproject manager (at least, one who knows how to delegate authority to his or her charges) might possess without dramatically impeding his or her job performance. The self-professed claim of being a "big picture" person is ascribing to yourself an attribute that is desirable not only for the position you're seeking but for others further up the chain.

For our purposes, another way to approach this question is to place the context of "weakness" not on yourself or your personal attributes but rather on your experience, something which is easily curable; an example is given below.

In general, this is an idiotic question, but you may find yourself asked it repeatedly, so be prepared and try not to grimace too much.

Suggested answer

"To date, I haven't had large project experience with a lot of desktop technologies, even though I've been working for a year on my own to overcome this lack of experience. I have my own PC at home and have been developing small- and medium-sized applications in CA-Clipper, which is what your organization uses, I believe, and I feel confident that the skills I've acquired will more than make up for the absence of workplace experience."

(*Note:* Your "weakness" is simply not having worked with a product or two in a workplace environment, and your self-training efforts have already gone a long way toward overcoming this.)

Question 5   What are you looking for in a position?

Behind the scenes of the question

The primary purpose of this question is to make sure that your personal objectives—short-term, long-term, or both—are not counter to the environment in which you're interviewing. If, say, you reply that you're looking for a position from which you can advance rapidly through the corporate hierarchy, gaining tremendous responsibility and power as you build a corporate empire worthy of a *Fortune* 500 CEO, but you're interviewing at a small manufacturing firm run by two brothers who come to work in jeans and flannel shirts and drink beer over lunch and in which there is no corporate hierarchy whatsoever, it would be fairly obvious that regardless of your qualifications, your career objectives are very unlikely to be met in that particular work environment.

Your answer should, if possible, be tailored to the environment in which you're interviewing, but don't lie; in the above situation, if you are indeed looking for a *Fortune* 500 bureaucracy-heavy organization in which you can play the corporate ladder-climbing game, you probably won't be very happy in a laid-back, mom-and-pop operation, regardless of the technology in use. Similarly, if you are most comfortable in an informal environment with a lack of formal structure—one in which all that matters is the results of your work, not how many interdepartmental task forces you chair—then you should think long and hard about pursuing a position in a major corporation, regardless of how "neat" the technology is with respect to the position for which you're interviewing. This goes back to the self-assessment process we discussed in Chap. 2; before you even get to an interview, you should be sure that this is a position which, if it were offered to you, you would accept and be happy with.

Suggested answer

"I'm looking for a position where I can do hands-on work with PC and LAN products. At ABC, I worked exclusively doing COBOL maintenance programming on mainframes, and I tried for several years to get into the groups doing client/server development on PCs. A position such as this one in which I can do just that is highly attractive to me."

(*Note:* Without overdoing it, you want to say that "this job—this one right here—has everything that I want; really!")

Question 6   Where do you see yourself in three to five years?

Behind the scenes of the question

This is another flaky question, given the unpredictability and uncertainty of career paths and other factors. When asked this question, I've always been tempted to shoot back, "It depends; can you guarantee that you folks are going to be in business in three to five years and tell me what projects you'll be doing and what technologies you'll be using?"

The goal of your answer is to demonstrate your flexibility. Avoid replies like "I plan to move on to a supervisory role and then a managerial position" or "just what I'll be doing if I'm hired for this job, doing PC software development." Stress that as organizational goals change, as the technology of information systems evolves, you are adaptable to whatever challenges await you.

Suggested answer

"It's hard to get a very accurate fix on, say, the five-year time frame. Five years ago I would have said I'd still be at ABC Conglomerates, not laid off and looking for a new position. In general I'd like to grow with your organization, whether it's working on new projects, investigating new hardware or software systems, working with customers, or whatever the organizational goals are over that time period. Hopefully, I'll be able to have some input to those objectives, and I think that I'm flexible enough and have broad enough experience that I can adapt to whatever changes occur over the next three to five years."

(*Note:* Without being too noncommittal, you've said that "wherever the trade winds blow, I'll be there.")

Question 7   Give me an example of overcoming a difficult problem in your past job and how you did that.

Behind the scenes of the question

The interviewer is trying to gauge your creativity and your ability to work your way through the nonroutine matters that inevitably come up in every type of job, whether hands-on or managerial. You should have several candidates for this answer, and use the one (or two) most applicable to this particular position.

Suggested answer

(*Note:* This is repeated from Chap. 3, when we discussed the proper context of responses to interview questions.)

"There was an occasion where the communications software for which I was responsible apparently malfunctioned, but there was nothing in the dump that indicated where the problem was because all of the registers had been corrupted by the abnormal termination. To run the debugging facility for our communications modules, we typically had to be in live, test-mode contact with the remote site, and the next comm test run wasn't scheduled until about two weeks later. During the time that we were analyzing the problem and trying to find any bugs in the code, it occurred again, and the CIO was getting pretty upset.

"I recommended that we take one of the other processes in the system—we had a multiprocess environment—and modify its code to dump the message that had caused the problem into the common area buffers and simulate the external communications interrupt, and all of our debugging facilities could be on. We tried this and it worked, and we found the problem later that day and fixed it immediately."

(Hint: As was noted in Chap. 3, avoid the temptation to use your reply to this question as a chance for some serious bragging and self-aggrandizement. Stick to a matter-of-fact response in which your wondrous efforts are apparent without colorful commentary telling how you personally saved the day.)

Question 8   Do you like to work by yourself or with others?

Behind the scenes of the question

Most of the time you are asked this question because the work environment for which you are being considered involves either a heavy amount of teamwork or a tremendous amount of solo work, and, therefore, your preferences as to the type of environment in which you function best are being divined.

On the one hand, if you've already determined the type of environment the organization with which you are interviewing employs (sometimes you are told up front, as in "our developers are expected to be members of a cohesive, finely tuned, well-oiled, blah, blah, team—how do you feel about working in this type of environment?"), it's best to provide an answer that indicates that (1) you are absolutely comfortable in whatever type of environment is present there, but (2) you are adaptable and, in fact, have succeeded in both teamwork-oriented and solo-oriented settings. This way, you don't appear either as incapable of working with little guidance (if you stress that you prefer working as a member of a closely knit team) or as a loner who may be difficult to get along with (if, on the other hand, you state a preference for solo work).

Suggested answer

"I've worked well in both types of environments. At ABC Conglomerates, I typically worked with minimal supervision once a project had been assigned to me, though I regularly kept my supervisor and peers up to date with my progress."

Question 9   How do you feel about hands-on work?

Behind the scenes of the question

The sole purpose of this question is to gauge how, if you are trying to move backwards from a supervisory or managerial role with no hands-on technical involvement to a position that is primarily hands-on, you feel about this. Are you comfortable taking what traditionally has been seen as a major step backwards in one's career, often the end of corporate ladder climbing?

Regardless of how you really feel about moving back into a hands-on technical position, you have to sell yourself as "really looking forward to this opportunity." Your answer can focus on

The opportunity to learn "exciting, new technology"

Having enough self-assurance that you feel comfortable doing what you've liked best during your career, except now with "new stuff" (PC hardware and software, LANs, etc.), and you couldn't care less what anyone else thinks about this type of career move

Or whatever else convinces the interviewer that you indeed are not viewing a career move in this direction as a failure of any sort—you would be proud and happy to accept this position if it were offered to you.

Suggested answer

"I gave that specific issue a great deal of thought when I began my job search following my layoff from ABC Conglomerates. I had several opportunities to move to a similar supervisory role at companies comparable to ABC, but given all that has transpired in the industry over the past few years, I didn't believe that these opportunities would be very stable or offer me what I really want out of a position. I've thoroughly enjoyed doing PC-based software development while I was training myself on my own time, and for the year that I was doing that while I was still at ABC, I wished almost every day that I could be doing that as part of my position there. The chance to do that type of development full-time would absolutely be satisfactory for me; in fact, I can't imagine a more satisfying job."

Question 10   Why do you want to work here?

Behind the scenes of the question

This is another question where your answer is unlikely to tilt the competition for a job in your favor, but the wrong answer could quickly take you out of the running. Try to avoid gushing about how wonderful the company/division/office is, how absolutely wonderful and peachy all the people are, or anything that sounds hollow, particularly if this is your first exposure to the company with which you're interviewing. Focus on the attractive aspects of the position, such as (1) the technology with which you'll work, (2) the project on which you'll work (how interesting it is, etc.), (3) that you've heard positive things about the company (if, indeed, you have; if not, don't lie), and anything else that makes it seem that you really want to work for that company doing that job.

Suggested answer

"From everything I've heard, this seems like it would be an ideal position. I've learned a lot about FoxPro development from my training work and have really liked using the product, and since your entire project is being done in FoxPro, this would be an excellent project. The company seems to be a great place to work, from what I've been told and what I've seen."

Question 11   What type of organization do you like?

Behind the scenes of the question

This question is somewhat related to the previous two questions. Its purpose is to gauge your suitability for the particular job—not necessarily from a technical point of view, but rather in terms of how well you'll fit into the organizational culture at this particular place. Perhaps your background, both as a worker and as a manager, is exclusively in strictly authoritarian, top-down, micromanaging environments with rigid lines of authority, and you actually feel most comfortable in such an organization. If this particular place is rather laid back with a flat organizational structure and very participative decision-making processes, you may feel out of place, particularly if you are in a leadership role and find others questioning your decisions and thought processes (and you have never had that happen before). By contrast, if you function best in a freewheeling, decentralized, mostly informal culture, finding yourself in a militaristic corporation with rigidly enforced working hours, weekly (sometimes daily) formal status reports, prolonged staff meetings, and other trappings of bureaucracy can make the technological shift you successfully undertake pale compared to the crushing autocratic burden.

(By the way, can you guess from the above text where my own preferences lie? I specifically included this question and the accompanying discussion because unless you are absolutely in need of a job quickly for financial or other reasons, you should take a long, hard look at the organizational culture into which you are headed. If you don't think you can survive in that type of environment, or if you worked in similar surroundings in the past and hated the experience, you might as well avoid the unpleasantness you no doubt will be facing very soon.)

Suggested answer

(Assuming that the company has a relatively loose organizational structure with a great deal of employee self-direction):

"I've always worked very well when I've been given a task and some basic information, and gone off with my team members and worked on the problem. We've always kept our manager informed as to our progress, but for the most part I've liked places where there hasn't been a lot of structured, day-to-day reporting of all work in progress, but that have been results-oriented."

Question 12   What have you disliked about past jobs?

Behind the scenes of the question

Like several of our previous sample questions, this one is intended to be a "weeding" question, looking for you to say that some characteristic that this particular organization possesses is distasteful to you. It's best to stick with generic statements that are more esoteric in nature rather than specifics like "an overbearing boss" or "impossible deadlines."

Suggested answer

"On two separate occasions, I've had projects on which I've worked for over two years be suddenly canceled. In one case it was due to an upper-ranks reorganization where our project was folded into another; it was sort of a power struggle between two vice presidents, and our guy lost, so our project funding was cancelled. The other time was when a new group director came into ABC Conglomerates and funded new projects that she wanted to do, and got the funding by canceling our product development. I know that corporate politics are part of the game, but it was disheartening in both cases to have the projects cancelled even though we were on schedule and would have delivered good systems."

(*Note:* Your answer concentrates on things beyond your control and your reluctant acceptance of those situations, and also slips in how you were still chugging along, staying on schedule, while the corporate intrigue was occurring.)

Question 13   What have you liked about past jobs?

Behind the scenes of the question

This question doesn't pose quite the trap that the previous one does, and it gives you a chance to profess your appreciation of characteristics that (how about that!) this company also has. Just try not to be too obvious.

Suggested answer

"When I was at XYZ, I was one of the first people trained in C programming, and I loved it. I got a chance to do new project development instead of the COBOL maintenance I had been doing, and to work with VAX systems instead of mainframes. I've always liked working with new technologies; that's made jobs enjoyable."

Question 14   What factors are important to you in a job?

Behind the scenes of the question

Here is another question with landmine potential. Even if, like many people, you are driven primarily by compensation, both salary and incentive pay (bonuses, profit sharing, etc.), it's not advisable to state that this is the primary factor. You can, of course, state that in an offhand way (see below) after you go through other factors such as new technologies, challenges, not being bored, etc.

Suggested answer

"There are a couple of things. I want to be challenged, to be given projects which I can really get into and do my best on. I prefer to be working with more or less state-of-the-art technology, and after what happened at ABC Conglomerates, where I was stuck doing mainframe work for so long and then suddenly laid off, I don't want something like that to happen again. Compensation is important, too; it's nice to be recognized for helping the company achieve its goals."

(Hint: Avoid corporate ladder-climbing goals like "the opportunity to advance quickly through the corporate hierarchy"; it makes you appear to be interested solely in promotions at the expense of the tasks at hand—and, for that matter, everything else of importance to the organization.)

Question 15   Tell me about client/server computing.

Behind the scenes of the question

This question provides an excellent transition from the questions of this chapter to those of the subsequent chapters, which are more technical in nature. A question (actually, a request) of this nature is designed to see how well you really know the general technology for which you're being considered. By "general technology" I mean client/server computing, object-oriented computing, CASE, reengineering and reverse engineering—gross-level groupings into which various products, standards, and other components fall.

In this specific case, an interviewer is mostly looking for red flags that indicate that you actually have little understanding of client/server computing, that most of your knowledge is from marketing hype and high-level overviews (articles, etc.). You want to avoid overblown claims like "client/server computing will replace all mainframes by the turn of the century" or "every company that moves to client/server computing from terminal-based mainframe systems saves at least 50 percent on its hardware and software maintenance costs within two years." In short, know what you're talking about, because you can be sure that your interviewer does.

Suggested answer

"There are a lot of aspects of client/server computing. When you look at trends like smaller-scale hardware components—PCs and workstations, as well as server systems—and the heterogeneity that comes from many different vendors providing products that fill certain needs, it's very difficult to construct centralized systems in a cost-effective manner, especially since users often want to mix and match hardware and software components. With client/server computing, the separation of the user-oriented functions—function requests, results reporting, that type of thing—from the back-end functions like database management and network services helps promote this mix-and-match approach to systems. When client/server computing first started, most products were homogeneous, with little interoperability with other products or other server functions. Now, mostly because of all of the standards activities going on, you have a greater degree of heterogeneity in operational client/server systems. In many cases, the mainframes and minicomputers remain in the environment, providing the server functions to PC and workstation front-ends."

(You can go on as long as you feel comfortable and as long as the interviewer's eyes aren't glazing over. The point is, stick to the facts as you know them, avoid marketing-like hype, and you'll do just fine, even if you have never personally worked in a client/server environment before!)

Question 16   How do you handle technical conflict?

Behind the scenes of the question

This question is actually a dual-edged one, and one which you must answer with a bit of caution. It is aimed primarily at computer professionals who have been in supervisory or technical lead positions and who have been in a position to make strategic and tactical recommendations to the decision makers concerning the technical direction of a project or product (although it *may* be asked of junior-level folks as well if they also were in such a position).

The interviewer wants to learn a couple of things. First, how do you handle having your ideas rebuffed? Do you rant and rave? Maybe you retire to your cubicle or office and pout. Obviously you wouldn't say this in an overt manner ("those managers were such idiots that I figured, fine, let them screw up the entire project; I never said another word about it!"), but you need to be careful that such an attitude doesn't peek through the words of your reply.

On the other hand, the position for which you're being considered may involve some degrees of teamwork and corporate politics; that is, you're expected to argue your position as best you can, but if the decision is made to go another way, you will do your best to carry out the directives.

The key is to appear to be forceful enough and thorough enough to have (1) researched your position as carefully as you could have, (2) defended your position as forcefully as possible, and (3) neither gloated in victory nor sulked in defeat.

Suggested answer

"We had this situation at XYZ Corp. when we were deciding among CASE architectures for the systems overhaul program. *My concern* was that the state of CASE technology, particularly *integrated CASE environments,* wasn't mature enough for a full-scale commitment, particularly with a mix-and-match approach to different products. I had proposed that a *more practical* solution would be to take several "best of breed" tools and either find off-the-shelf integration products (*I had come across several during my research*) or develop our own interoperability mechanisms, possibly using an export/import model or maybe live links, *whatever was most appropriate for any set of tools.*

"What happened, though, was the management decided to go with the ambitious approach, the one using the ABCXYZ framework. *I was fairly concerned about this direction and voiced those concerns,* but I was overruled and I *helped the project as best I could* given the potential pitfalls. It turned out that the capabilities were less than had been advertised, and about a year and a half later we wound up going back to the drawing board and starting over. *This time, they started by using the approach I had originally proposed,* and the last I heard from the folks there was that the program was actually on schedule and within budget."

Key components of your answer

1. *My concern*   These seemingly benign words tell the interviewer that when it comes to "really neat technical stuff" (such as integrated CASE, in this sample question), you actually put some thought into the matter; you don't just jump in head first with the attitude that "wow, I get to play with all these really cool new toys!"

2. *integrated CASE environments*   You're merely indicating that you are aware of trends such as I-CASE. If this area is on the drawing board for the company with which you're interviewing, it may pique their interest in you even further. (A personal note: I've had several interviews during my career where I brought up technical areas which hadn't appeared in the job announcement or newspaper ad but turned out to be of interest to that company and sparked a long series of questions in that area. In most cases, this helped keep me in consideration for those positions.)

3. *more practical*   Related to the first point above, you are letting the interviewer know that your focus with respect to technical decision making is heavily weighted toward success in the mission at hand, not wild-eyed exploration of emerging technology (unless, of course, you're interviewing for a research-oriented position, but these days even those types of jobs are more oriented toward the likelihood of tangible results than toward "just checking out the landscape").

4. *I had come across several during my research*   You have the basic foundation not only to come up with an initial recommendation, but also to pursue the issue by researching as many external sources as possible.

5. *whatever was most appropriate for any set of tools*   Related to point 3 above; not only are your thought processes oriented toward practical, working solutions, but you are also cognizant of situational considerations; no solution is best for every possible environment or setting.

6. *I was fairly concerned about this direction and voiced those concerns*   You aren't afraid to voice your opinion when you believe you're right. If there are follow-up questions about how you did so, make sure that you stress that you were diplomatic yet forceful (assuming, of course, that that was the case; if you actually *did* throw a temper tantrum or sulk, avoid the subject as best you can...and learn from your mistakes!).

7. *helped the project as best I could*   You're just the best darn team player there could possibly be; you gave your all even though the direction wasn't what you had recommended. No hard feelings, eh, mate? (Hint: Don't let your answer seem too fake. You're human, and the interviewer knows that you're human—just let him or her know that you aren't the kind of person who sabotages efforts or doesn't support them when you don't get your way.)

8. *This time, they started by using the approach I had originally proposed*   (Hint: Make absolutely sure that your "victory dance" statement doesn't have an "I told them so, and I was right" tone to it!") It turns out that your recommendation was right, after all.

Software and Systems Development in the Desktop Environment

As we noted earlier in this book, the distinctions between the mainframe- and/or minicomputer-based development models with which you are probably familiar and those that are most applicable to desktop computing go beyond the obvious differences in capacity, performance, and other factors between the old and new technology worlds. Simply put, the methodologies and techniques that have commonly been used in large-scale systems development efforts are, for the most part, out of place in the desktop computing arena. Whether it is your choice of languages and development systems or the actual life cycle methodology that you employ, it is likely that an interviewer will try to gauge not only your technical competence in PCs, LANs, and other newer computing areas but also the process by which you would go about developing systems.

In this chapter, we'll look at some of the questions you are likely to be asked in this area, presenting the types of answers which are likely to instill confidence in your interviewers that you won't be bringing old, tired development techniques to the technology with which you'll be working.

Question 1 How would you develop a business applications system that involves PCs and LAN technology?

Behind the scenes of the question

This *very* open-ended question is designed to gauge the methodologies, techniques, and development systems that you would employ in the environment mentioned in the question. The interviewer is probably trying to gauge whether you would approach a PC-LAN system the same way you would a mainframe- or minicomputer-based system, with a prolonged waterfall-oriented development life cycle (e.g., the requirements phase is worked on until it is completed, and it then feeds into specification and design, which are in turn worked on until they are completed; then development commences, and so on).

As we noted earlier in this book, the desktop computing world—particularly systems involving PCs—is best served by spiral-oriented methodologies, in which rapid prototyping and development of proof-of-concept pilot systems occurs, using the most highly productive development environments possible. Your answer should reflect this understanding.

Suggested answer

"Most of the projects that I worked on at ABC Conglomerates *had long-drawn-out development methodologies,* and usually by the time the system was fielded, many of the requirements had changed, and the users often wanted something very different from what they received. In a PC-LAN environment, I would pursue a methodology more conducive to *rapidly producing working prototypes* which could then be enhanced and ruggedized to meet the user community's operational needs. Instead of using a 3GL like COBOL, which we used at ABC, I would find it far more productive to use some type of *4GL or CASE-based generation system, with *screen and forms generators* built in. The PC products with which I've worked allow me to create screens and forms much faster than by calling system routines from a 3GL program. By getting something out there very quickly, you can get *the user community's buy-in* up front and make sure that you meet their requirements."

Key components of your answer

1. *had long-drawn-out development methodologies*   You tell the interviewer that you recognize the deficiencies in traditional development methodologies, and that you are easily adaptable to new ways of doing business.

2. *rapidly producing working prototypes*   You understand that the purpose of software and systems development is to support some type of business function, not coding for the sake of coding, and that time is of the essence with respect to development.

3. *4GL...screen and forms generators*   You are aware that there are

more alternatives to the problem of development platforms and systems than just programming languages, and that in the desktop world there is often a heavy reliance on such tools.

4. *the user community's buy-in*   Related to point 2 above; it is extremely important to have user involvement in the development process, and you aren't to be viewed as a "computing bigot," one who would put the wonders of technology above user-oriented functionality.

Question 2   How would you approach a systems integration project?

Behind the scenes of the question

In many PC-oriented environments, the primary activity of computer professionals is the integration of off-the-shelf components to create a functioning system. The interviewer is trying to determine how you would approach such a project—would you fall back on coding and software development rather than solve problems with off-the-shelf components?

Suggested answer

"The driving factor is the *users' requirements,* as the system must support the business function; this isn't really very different from a development-oriented project. Once the requirements have been determined and *validated,* I would conduct a search to see what commercial systems are available for that particular area. I'd look at some of the *on-line databases* like CompuServe, and I'd try to find out as much information as I could about off-the-shelf solutions. One of the factors I'd use to evaluate the candidates is how *customizable* each product is, since there is likely to be some variance between what is needed in-house and the product features.

"I'd also look at factors such as the *other systems* with which that particular component had to *integrate,* what *standards* are supported by the product, and things like that."

Key components of your answer

1. *users' requirements*   As with software development, you understand that information systems are designed to support some business function.

2. *validated*   It's important not only to gather user requirements,

but also to validate them, since what you first discover may be either erroneous or incomplete.

3. *on-line databases* You know the places to go to get current, up-to-date information about commercial products.

4. *customizable* You understand that there are likely to be some business functions that aren't directly supported by an off-the-shelf system, and the flexibility of commercial packages is an important factor. Software and computer systems should be tailored to fit a business's operations, not the other way around.

5. *other systems...integrate* Few applications or subsystems stand alone; they usually need to work with other I.S. components, and you are capable of handling the "big picture" aspect.

6. *standards* You recognize the importance of standards, even in the desktop computing world.

Question 3   What do you consider to be the major component areas of an information system?

Behind the scenes of the question

First, this question is somewhat unclear, *as will be many of those that you will be asked during an interview.* Don't be afraid to ask for a clarification! It's best to make sure that you are answering the question the interviewer *did* ask rather than your incorrect interpretation of that question.

In general, the interviewer is looking to see if you understand that modern, distributed information systems are composed of a number of *service areas,* each serving some particular cohesive need. Service areas include[1]

- Data management
- System services (e.g., operating systems calls)
- Graphics
- User interface
- Communications
- Programming

---

[1]From A. Simon, *Enterprise Computing,* Bantam Books/Intertext, New York, 1992, p. 166.

■ Data interchange

Your answer should reflect your knowledge of these particular areas, as well as the importance of standards to each area.

Suggested answer

"With distributed systems, you have a greater reliance on *standards-based* services than you do in centralized environments like the mainframe systems we used at ABC Conglomerates. You have areas like data management, which includes both user data and *metadata*. There are also service areas for networks and communications, graphics, user interfaces, programming—programming areas are standardized language bindings to help promote *portability*—and operating system services. Also, if you have a *heterogeneous* environment, then data interchange is very important."

Key components of your answer

1. *standards-based*   You understand the importance of avoiding a hodgepodge of programming interfaces, and recognize the role of standards.

2. *metadata*   Not only are user data important, but so are metadata, particularly for interapplication and intercomponent cooperability.

3. *portability*   Use of widely accepted standards will lead to portability; this is important in the desktop environment as well as with larger systems.

4. *heterogeneous*   You are telling the interviewer that you are aware of the mix-and-match nature of desktop computing, using products from numerous vendors and having those products work with one another.

Question 4   How would you develop an application to be portable?

Behind the scenes of the question

Software developers from mainframe and, for the most part, minicomputer environments have traditionally been little concerned with application portability. Despite lip service toward areas like abstraction layers, most software developed for those environments has been tightly (nearly irrevocably) coupled with the underlying hardware and operating system platforms.

In desktop computing environments, portability is a key aspect of all systems development efforts. The interviewer is trying to determine (1) that you recognize the importance of portability, and (2) how you would proceed in developing portable applications.

Suggested answer

"A great deal of portability is achieved through *good software development practices* that are applicable to PC and workstation environments as well as larger systems. These practices include modularized code, abstraction layers above system-dependent services, and other things like that. Using *standards-based services* whenever possible makes applications more portable from one platform to another than if system-specific services are used. There are also *multienvironment tools* that can be used to develop generic applications that can be instantiated in different manners on different platforms. An example of this tool is XVT, through which a generic graphical user interface can be created that can then be instantiated as Microsoft Windows, MOTIF, Macintosh, or another GUI."

Key components of your answer

1. *good software development practices*   It's beneficial to emphasize that even though you may have been a FORTRAN mainframe programmer in the past, you are well aware of software engineering principles.

2. *standards-based services*   As with our previous sample question, you should emphasize that you understand the importance of standards (though, as we'll note in question 6 in this chapter, you don't want to go overboard preaching the wonders of standards).

3. *multienvironment tools*   You emphasize that you have kept up to date with development tools of all types, including service-specific generators (e.g., a generic GUI development environment such as XVT, from which multiple instances of GUI managers can be created for different environments).

Question 5   What do you know about CASE in PC environments?

Behind the scenes of the question

Like "tell me about client/server computing" in Chap. 8, this question probably involves more than just gauging how much you know about various CASE tools. It is also designed to see if you can discern the difference between real functionality and capabilities and marketing hype. CASE has been highly touted since the early 1980s, but for the most part it has fallen well short of the vendor hype and user community expectations.

Your answer should reflect what you do know about CASE, but should steer well clear of superlatives and unsubstantiated claims of productivity boosts, rapid systems generation, etc.

Suggested answer

"It's interesting that in the past year or so, CASE seems to be gaining new life, particularly in the PC environments. The first decade or so really wasn't much to speak about, especially with PC-based case tools. The hardware environments didn't support *large designs or complex graphics, model verification and validation, intermodel mapping,* and other capabilities.

With a lot of lessons learned from the first couple of generations of tools, plus all of the *newer powerful, high-capacity PCs,* many organizations are taking a second look at PC-based CASE. There are a lot of powerful, highly acclaimed tools that either handle the full life cycle or are able to plug into an *integrated CASE* framework."

Key components of your answer

1. *large designs or complex graphics, model verification and validation, intermodel mapping*   In the body of your answer, you are telling the interviewer that you understand that CASE is more than just "pretty pictures" representing designs; rather it has a great deal of underlying semantics behind the concept.

2. *newer powerful, high-capacity PCs*   You tell the interviewer that you understand that all PCs are not created equal, and that tremendous strides have been made in recent years in putting a great deal of computing power on the desktop, power that is usable for tasks far beyond basic word processing and spreadsheet management.

3. *integrated CASE*   You are up to date with what is going on in the CASE world, including multiproduct integrated environments that use frameworks and platforms to cooperate with one another.

Question 6   What role do standards play in systems development?

Behind the scenes of the question

With several of the earlier questions, your answer might include references to the growing role of standards in information systems. As with the previous question, though, it's important to let the interviewer know that you are aware of the difference between hype and usable I.S. assets, and of the applicability of standards to desktop environments.

Much has been made of standards like the ISO Open Systems Interconnection (OSI) Reference Model, a seven-layer set of communications protocols designed to allow systems to communicate with one another. It's important to note that the OSI Reference Model has been under development for nearly 15 years[2] and in recent years has been supplanted as the open communications protocol of choice by TCP/IP-based environments. As with client/server computing, CASE, and other areas like object-oriented computing, avoid letting your answer degenerate into a marketing pitch. Likewise, your answer should reflect your understanding that not all standards-compliant products are identical to one another in terms of that compliance (for example, SQL-based database management systems) and that "plug and play" interoperability is still more of a goal than a reality.

Suggested answer

"Standards are very important to most modern I.S. environments, particularly *heterogeneous* ones. It's important, though, to have a good idea of the viability and maturity of the various standards when you select them. You have some, like *SQL,* which has been around in product form since the early 1980s and standardized since the mid-1980s, that are fairly mature. You have others, like the *OSI Reference Model,* which are very complex and still not widely adopted.

"Another issue is that not all standards-compliant products can seamlessly interoperate with one another, and *gateways and other interface mechanisms* are often needed. If you look at SQL database products, for example, you have related standards such as *the SQL CLI effort* through which client/server SQL database products will hopefully be able to work together. It's important to *evaluate products*

---

[2]Ibid., p. 232.

to see how compliant with standards they are, and to make sure that in any given environment products which are supposed to work together really do."

Key components of your answer

1. *heterogeneous*   You show the interviewer that you understand that many systems are constructed using products from different vendors.

2. *SQL...OSI Reference Model*   You let the interviewer know that you are familiar with several types of standards programs, even if you have yet to personally work with them.

3. *gateways and other interface mechanisms*   The interviewer learns that you have a realistic view of standards-based products in terms of the likelihood that another level of integration will be required. Additionally, related to the systems integration question above, you reemphasize your understanding that distributed, heterogeneous systems are usually constructed using various types of integration mechanisms.

4. *the SQL CLI effort*   You tell the interviewer that you track not only standards efforts but corollary efforts designed to help standards-based products work together more seamlessly.

5. *evaluate products*   You are not susceptible to marketing hype from either vendors or standards communities; instead, you want to closely evaluate products for applicability to your particular needs.

Question 7   What do you know about Chicago?

Behind the scenes of the question

The interviewer isn't asking for the names of good restaurants near O'Hare Airport or if Michael Jordan is really going to help the White Sox this year.

Chicago is the next generation of Microsoft Windows (not to be confused with Cairo, Microsoft's object-oriented operating system project). The interviewer primarily wants to see how well you stay up to date with *emerging* desktop computing technology (at least in terms of familiarity). It may be that that particular organization is planning on moving its entire suite of PCs to Chicago when it is commercially released, and wants to see if you have any great insight into the matter. Or it could just be a matter-of-course question, to see what your opinion is either from personal experience (maybe you had been involved in beta testing the product) or from what you've read.

Suggested answer

"That's the follow-on operating system to Microsoft Windows 3.1; it's one of the operating system projects going on at Microsoft along with *Windows NT* and *Cairo,* their object-oriented operating system. There's some discussion about whether Chicago will ship in 1994 or 1995, but it's expected that about half of Windows users will upgrade to it reasonably soon after it's released.

"There are a number of *new features* that are supposed to be in Chicago: a status bar at the bottom of the screen, a distributed data file utility called Explorer, a recycling bin that's supposed to be similar to the Macintosh trash can (files can be removed but not physically deleted), and a briefcase icon, which helps provide configuration management between desktop and laptop systems."

Key components of your answer

General hint. If your information is coming primarily from journals or other periodical sources, be careful about what you state as the unequivocal truth. A specific example with respect to this particular question: Two articles about Chicago appeared in issues of *Computerworld* only a few weeks apart (see References below). In one, there was a reference to "the beta product" of Chicago and quotes from beta testers. The other, published two weeks *later,* noted that the beta version of Chicago was not yet available.

Even though it's not the end of the free world as we know it if you make a statement during an interview that, for example, a particular product or test version is not yet available and it turns out that the organization actually has a copy in-house, it still doesn't reflect favorably on the currency of your knowledge. No one should be expected to know everything about every product, of course, including details of pricing and availability, but you don't want to be caught during an interview (or, for that matter, on the job) making *authoritative* statements about items, only to have someone know that you are incorrect. If you aren't absolutely sure of a particular item, either defer discussion or at the very least qualify your remarks with things like "I read that..." or "I've heard that...."

In general, the sample answer above indicates that (1) you know about not only this particular product but also similar efforts (the references to *Windows NT* and *Cairo*), and (2) you have some idea of the *new features* that are expected to be included.

(As an aside, I'm not sure which of the two articles was correct, nor does it really matter—as noted above, I would not recommend making any authoritative statements solely on the basis of reading material. Besides, they could *both* be correct; perhaps, as of the date of writing Chicago was in *internal* field testing and the first article was referring to sources within Microsoft, but there was no external field test available to outside organizations. The point is that you *cannot*—repeat, *cannot*—determine the complete set of facts from two quarter-page articles, so don't do something foolish in the course of an interview and appear to have some inside knowledge that you've simply picked up from five minutes' worth of reading. You are very likely to wind up sabotaging an otherwise-smooth interview process.)

References, and for further information

E. Scannell and M. Fitzgerald, "Chicago Chock-Full of Features," *Computerworld,* Feb. 21, 1994, p. 16.

J. Gantz, "Chicago: Will Users Buy Into Microsoft's Plans?" *Computerworld,* March 7, 1994, p. 35.

Question 8   Can you tell me how you would use wireless technology if you were putting together a system today?

Behind the scenes of the question

In addition to the stated purpose of this question (how would you do a particular "something"), the interviewer also wants to try to gauge your perspective on reality with respect to heavily hyped technology. You want to avoid describing a system that would be more appropriately developed in, say, 1998 when you are discussing the 1994 time frame.

Suggested answer

"There's a lot of activity going on in wireless technology now, both from the communications end and with *mobile applications.* Basically, you have a client/server paradigm for mobile applications, with the mobile devices being the clients connected via wireless technology to various types of servers, but the application models are *different from those of static client/server environments.* Most wireless applications today are primarily *file transfer–oriented or involve store-*

and-forward electronic mail, but there is a growing trend toward try-ing to do more real-time applications.

"I'd look at some of the *off-the-shelf development environments,* such as those from a company called Client Server Technology—it has a product called *AirClient* which is supposed to be available soon that helps build a *rule base for managing mobile, distributed client sys-tems.* One of the issues with mobile applications is that the clients are in unpredictable locations, so *transaction and query models must be adapted* to the nomadic nature. There's a lot of research going on in this area right now."

Key components of your answer

1. *mobile applications...different from those of static client / server environments* You indicate that you realize that mobile applica-tions have different characteristics from static ones, and that the technology from the latter does not necessarily translate well to the former.

2. *file transfer–oriented or involve store-and-forward electronic mail* You've got to crawl before you walk. You understand that ambi-tious, "do everything" programs are likely to be doomed to failure or at least major setbacks. It's best, in this particular case, to get the basic functionality of the mobile computing environment up and running and do "the simple things" first. *Then* go for the ambi-tious efforts. Answering the specific question you were asked, you are noting that the predominant kinds of mobile applications today are somewhat limited, and that you may very well focus your efforts on those areas or, at best, areas which are slightly more sophisticated (but not orders of magnitude more so).

3. *off-the-shelf development environments* You indicate that you would use as many productivity-enhancing items as possible, including developmental environments tailored to particular envi-ronments such as mobile applications.

4. *AirClient...rule base for managing mobile, distributed client sys-tems* Related to point 3 above, you are even familiar with one (or more) of these systems and what it does. Be careful, though, as with our previous question about Chicago: don't go overboard with your answer.

5. *transaction and query models must be adapted* You are also aware of the research directions in this area.

References, and for further information

E. Booker, "Tool Kit Aimed at Wireless Apps," *Computerworld,* March 7, 1994, p. 74.

Question 9   Assume that you're developing GUI-based applications. How much training do you think is necessary for end users?

Behind the scenes of the question

The interviewer is probably trying to determine your perspective on software usability. While it's unarguable that GUI environments are easier to use than the command line that most mainframe and mini-computer professionals have used (particularly at the operating system level), it shouldn't be assumed that GUI applications are automatically and immediately usable by the entire user community (or, for that matter, the development community if the GUI applications are system applications such as visual language facilities).

Suggested answer

"Some degree of training is needed for most applications, especially *to get the full range of functionality.* Even with GUI environments, you may have, say, a *menu bar* with seven or eight items, but each of those may have seven or eight entries, and some of those may have *submenus.* Then you may also have several *toolbars* with 30 or 40 graphical buttons.

"Even with *on-line help* and easy-to-use documentation, it's probably desirable to have a least several days of training for end users, especially those who may never have used a computer before. You can't assume that everyone even knows how to use a mouse or the basics of a GUI, and maybe these users would need "pretraining training" in the basics of PC usage. I would say that for most applications you don't need two-week courses like you would for something like learning a programming language, but at least several days' worth of training can't hurt.

Key components of your answer

1. *some degree of training...to get the full range of functionality* You believe that even for "simple" applications, at least some training is necessary. Further, the purpose of the training is not to have two or three days away from one's job, but to learn how to *most effectively* use an application (i.e., the goal is productivity, and if training leads to productivity, it is important).

2. *menu bar...submenus...toolbars*   As a "bonus answer," you indicate that you are aware not only of the acronym "GUI" but also of what some of the components of GUI applications and environments are.

3. *on-line help*   A very important part of GUI applications is on-line help, and you (1) acknowledge this, but (2) realize that its primary role (for many users) is posttraining quick reference, not on-the-fly learning. On-line help is usually not a good substitute for training, whether classroom- or computer-based (and you may wish to work computer-based training into your answer if you have familiarity with course preparation).

10

Hardware

In this chapter, we'll look at some of the questions you may be asked during an interview through which you must communicate your understanding of desktop computing hardware environments. Specifically, an interviewer must be convinced that you don't simply divide the hardware world into gross-level categories of mainframes, midrange systems, and PCs.

The PC world is once again becoming complicated, after nearly a decade when you could pretty much divide it into two camps: IBM PC compatibles (DOS and later Windows systems) and Apple Macintosh systems. Now we have PowerPC and Alpha systems, not to mention a mix-and-match approach to operating environments (discussed in the next chapter), such as Windows NT and NextStep, and the underlying hardware platforms.

Let's look at some of the questions you may find yourself being asked.

Question 1   We're looking at working with Alpha PCs. Do you know anything about them?

Behind the scenes of the question

This is a fairly straightforward question that gives you an opportunity to demonstrate that you have kept up to date with the latest developments in the desktop world, even if you haven't used the products yet. Further, it gives you an opportunity to demonstrate that you can go beyond the superficial and get down to the nitty-gritty with respect to emerging technology.

Suggested answer

"I have some familiarity with Alpha systems; I've been doing *a lot of reading* about the systems, and I've received *product literature* from Digital Equipment about the products. Right now, there are two different Alpha-based PCs, one which runs UNIX and another which runs Windows NT. Both use the 21064 Alpha 64-bit RISC chip, but there are some differences between the products.

"The Model 300, which is the UNIX box, has a 64-bit data bus, while the AXP 150—the Windows NT machine—has a 128-bit external data bus and seems to do a better job of making use of the Alpha chip's power. The Model 300 uses the DEC TurboChannel expansion bus for peripherals, while the AXP 150 is similar to an Intel-based EISA system.

"Both systems are pretty *pricey* now, though; the UNIX Model 300 system is almost $10,000, while the AXP 150 is around $6800. As with most hardware systems, though, prices should come down at some point."

Key components of your answer

1. *a lot of reading*   You let the interviewer know that you are serious about learning as much as possible about desktop computing technology, even if you aren't currently using a specific product.

2. *product literature*   Related to the item above, you also show self-initiative, contacting a vendor to get up-to-date product information. In the PC and desktop world, this is often expected of systems developers—much more so than among traditional mainframe programmers.

3. *pricey*   You have some understanding of the cost of technology, and are capable of conducting cost/benefit analyses as necessary. You aren't impressed by technology for the sake of technology.

References, and for further information

R. Grehan, "A Tale of Two Alphas," *Byte,* December 1992, pp. 169–172.

Question 2   How would you choose a PC from all of the brands available?

Behind the scenes of the question

Take the 486-based PC world: There are hundreds of products from which you can choose, with different clock speeds, expansion options, and other characteristics. The interviewer is trying to determine several things, including (1) how much you know about different types of PCs and how to distinguish one from another, and (2) your discovery and evaluation processes.

Suggested answer

"There are a lot of factors that must be considered. First, you *have different types of 486 processors*—SX, DX, DX2, all running at various clock speeds. At present, for *business use* it's advisable to go with a DX2 66-MHz system unless the PC will only be used for very light work. I was *reading* a review in a recent issue of *Byte* in which 90 different systems were evaluated, and it was interesting how much *prices* have been dropping at the high end, not to mention how much better *performance* is getting.

"For the most part, you can probably assume that prices will keep dropping, and that at *any given time* you will be able to purchase systems that perform better for less money than those which were bought only a couple of months earlier. I would keep track of which systems are rated most highly and are most cost-effective so that at the point when *new stations are to be added to the environment,* I could concentrate my purchases in that area."

Key components to your answer

1. *have different types of 486 processors*   You understand not only that, say, 486 systems are different from 386 systems in terms of capabilities, but that there are different types of 486 processors as well.

2. *business use*   You understand that PCs for business use should be evaluated according to different criteria from those for home use.

3. *reading*   Again, you stay up to date with rapidly changing technology.

4. *prices...performance*   These are some of the evaluation factors you would use.

5. *any given time...new stations are to be added to the environment* Unlike with mainframes or minicomputers, purchases of new PCs are not a major event. In PC-intensive enterprises, new stations are continually being added to the overall system. Because of this phased approach, you can, at any given time, probably purchase systems that are less expensive *and* more powerful than those which you had previously bought. Therefore, on an iterative, phased basis, you can continually upgrade your PC-based I.S. environment.

References, and for further information

R. Fox, "90 High-Speed 486 Systems," *Byte,* December 1993, pp. 176–201.

Question 3   How much memory would you put onto a 486 PC?

Behind the scenes of the question

In addition to the obvious aspect, wanting to see what your answer is, the interviewer is also looking to see if you understand the situational nature that drives the answer to this question. If your PC is running DOS applications, you can get by with significantly less memory than if you are running Microsoft Windows. Likewise, Windows requires less memory than UNIX or Windows NT. Your response should reflect your understanding of the conditions that drive the answer.

Suggested answer

"It *depends on what operating environment* the PC is going to be running. For DOS applications you should look at 4 megabytes of memory, while Windows-based environments should have at least 8 megabytes. I'd put on even more for *UNIX* applications, especially if they are computationally intensive, and I'd look at 16 megabytes for *Windows NT.*"

Key components of your answer

1. *depends on what operating environment*   You understand that this hardware characteristic is driven by a systems software factor, specifically what operating environment is going to be used. Not all operating environments have the same characteristics, and you recognize this.

2. *UNIX...Windows NT*   You understand that PCs go beyond DOS and Windows (and, for that matter, Macintosh System 7), and in today's information systems often include complex operating systems such as UNIX and Windows NT.

References, and for further information

R. Fox, "90 High-Speed 486 Systems," *Byte,* December 1993, pp. 176–201.

Question 4   What disk drive capacity do you feel is right for a PC?

Behind the scenes of the question

As with the previous question, the interviewer is looking to see if you understand the situational nature of PCs. You don't want to be continually upgrading PCs' disk drives, nor do you want a tremendous amount of unused (and likely never to be used) space. When you consider that some I.S. environments have thousands of PCs, wasted money in terms of disk capacity that was purchased but will never be used can quickly add up.

Suggested answer

"Like memory, it depends on the type of *operating environment,* plus there are additional factors such as the *applications* which will be run. DOS environments should have at least 100 megabytes of storage, while double that—200 megabytes—is best for Microsoft Windows. For Windows NT, probably 300 megabytes should be right.

"With regard to the application type, if you're going to run database applications that will manage large databases, that will probably require even more capacity."

Key components to your answer

1. *operating environment* As with memory capacity, you recognize the situational nature of your answer.

2. *applications* You understand that different applications have different storage requirements. Management of large volumes of information, particularly if the PC will be configured as a network-based file server, will probably require significant disk capacity, perhaps more than 1 gigabyte.

References, and for further information

R. Fox, "90 High-Speed 486 Systems," *Byte,* December 1993, pp. 176–201.

Question 5   We're looking at installing several color printers on our LAN. What are some of the tradeoffs of the different types of color printers?

Behind the scenes of the question

Again, this is a relatively straightforward question, but representative of the type of things which will define your desktop computing job. Very often you will be asked to make recommendations about what types of peripheral devices should be purchased, and you will have very little to go on other than general guidelines like "we want color printing." Your answer should reflect both your technical under-standing and the process by which you would perform your evalua-tion and make your recommendations.

Suggested answer

"There are a couple of different color printing options, and the choice *depends on cost factors and what the output is going to be used for.* At the low end, you have *ink-jet* printers, but you often wind up with runny ink and paper wrinkles; besides, they are rather slow. There are some new technologies to help prevent the running ink, so the quality should get better there in the near future. Color *laser* printers are also slow and are rather expensive, and right now there's only one desktop system available. *Thermal-transfer* printers are expensive but dropping in price, but you sometimes have to use special paper. There are also *dye-diffusion* color printers, but these are around $8000.

"I'd look at the purpose of the printers. If they're mostly for in-house use, doing things like printing negative balances on spread-sheets in red ink and preparing color interdepartment newsletters, then a high-quality ink-jet printer would probably be sufficient. If they're for documents that are going outside the company that must be top-quality, then it's probably worth investing in a more expensive technology."

Key components of your answer

1. *depends on cost factors and what the output is going to be used for* High-quality color printers are "neat," but the cost-effectiveness is determined by the purpose of the device. You understand this, and you make this clear to the interviewer.

2. *ink-jet...laser...thermal-transfer...dye-diffusion* You understand that the category "color printer," much like "personal computer" or "workstation," can be broken down into several subcategories, and you are astute enough to recognize the tradeoffs among the vari-ous technologies.

References, and for further information

R. Fox, "90 High-Speed 486 Systems," *Byte,* December 1993, pp. 176–201.

Question 6   Do you know the difference between SCSI-1 and SCSI-2 systems?

Behind the scenes of the question

This is a straightforward question, one that is representative of the type of job problem you might encounter when you are required to decide between several technical options.

Suggested answer

"SCSI-1 and SCSI-2 are *compatible* with one another, except that SCSI-2 has some *new modes of operation,* things like the 10 megabytes per second Fast SCSI-2. SCSI-2 also uses a high-density *50-pin connector* rather than the 25-pin connectors of SCSI-1. Supposedly, all SCSI-1 devices should work with SCSI-2 controllers, but there are some *minor glitches* on some devices in areas like *arbitration,* when multiple devices try to get onto the SCSI bus at the same time. If you're going to be connecting a device or two to a PC, then SCSI-1 devices are OK; for *multiple different devices,* though, you probably want to go with SCSI-2."

Key components of your answer

1. *compatible...new modes of operation*   You understand the differences and similarities.

2. *50-pin connector*   Mainframe and minicomputer programmers typically don't deal much with connectors and cables, aside from those which are connected to their display terminals. In the desktop computing world, however, you often find yourself hooking devices up to one another, and it's important to know what types of cables and connectors are required.

3. *minor glitches*   Even though SCSI-1 devices are supposed to run flawlessly under SCSI-2 controllers, in reality there are minor problems, and you understand this.

4. *arbitration*   Peripheral support involves more than just hooking up devices and forgetting about them; if problems occur, it is often your job to track down the problem and analyze it. By understanding that SCSI systems perform arbitration, and that this is one of the areas in which some incompatibility may occur, you can save yourself hours of frustration as you try to figure out why something doesn't work correctly.

5. *multiple different devices*   Finally, as with color printers and other hardware subjects we've discussed, you understand the factors that will drive the decision that must be made with respect to type of hardware.

References, and for further information

J. Allweis, "Cabling and Compatibility," *PC Upgrade,* 2(5): 12–18, 1993.

Question 7　We're looking at Macintosh systems, but we're totally confused about the different choices. What do you know about the different types of Macintosh computers?

Behind the scenes of the question

This could be a straightforward question, with the interviewer really asking for assistance and information. At one time (the early days of the Macintosh family), the product line was relatively simple to understand. In recent years, it has gotten very complex and, some would argue, convoluted. Recently, Apple streamlined the product line, creating four different categories of Macintosh systems. By detailing your understanding of Macintosh technology, not just conceptually but with respect to where the product line is headed, you can give the interviewer confidence that if they add Macintosh systems to their environment, *you* are the person to whom they should look for assistance.

Suggested answer

"Apple now has four different product lines of Macintosh systems— the *Performas, LCs, Quadras,* and *PowerBooks.* Performas are single-box systems designed primarily for home use, and are sold through computer superstores and retailers like Sears and Wal-Mart. LCs are for the educational market. The ones *most pertinent to your company* will probably be the Quadras and maybe the PowerBooks, if you make use of laptop systems. The Quadra systems not only have LocalTalk network interfaces, but also *Ethernet,* through which you can interface with other PCs. You can get *low-end* Quadras for barely over $1000, with a *high-end,* 68040-based system with 8 megabytes of RAM running between $3800 and $5500."

Key components of your answer

1. *Performas, LCs, Quadras,* and *PowerBooks*　You know the different types of systems and the purposes for which they are intended.

2. *most pertinent to your company*　Further, you know which lines to concentrate on in any systems selection efforts on the interviewer's company's behalf.

3. *Ethernet*   Macintosh proponents are often accused of being out of the mainstream of "normal" PC technology, including networking capabilities. You understand the importance of Ethernet to most organizations that make use of desktop computing.

4. *low-end...high-end*   Even within the family that you would target for systems selection, there are many different products; you know the pricing and characteristics differences between the various systems within that family.

References, and for further information
R. Ito, "And Then There Were 4," *MacUser,* December 1993, pp. 92–99.

Question 8   We're developing multimedia applications. What do you know about multimedia?

Behind the scenes of the question

This is a relatively straightforward question, but one which is too broad. It is recommended that you ask the interviewer to narrow his or her focus (not in those words, but perhaps with a qualifying question like "There's a lot of different areas...storage, audio, video. Which would you like me to elaborate on?"). Assuming that the focus of the question is narrowed to sound, you would concentrate on the MIDI specification and its applicability.

Suggested answer

"There's a de facto standard known as *MIDI*—that's the Musical Instrument Digital Interface—which defines a serial interface for connections *between computers and musical instruments and synthesizers.* The standard identifies hardware capabilities as understood by both sender and receiver; there are 128 sound effects, plus musical instruments and percussion sounds. There are *sound boards* that support the standard, so it's not too difficult to add music and sound to the applications that you're developing."

(Note: You could elaborate on MIDI, the various hardware characteristics, and other areas if appropriate; in fact, if the job for which you are interviewing deals primarily with multimedia data, you should be prepared to discuss MIDI aspects at length.)

Key components of your answer

1. *MIDI*   If you will be expected to work in a computerized audio environment, you will have to know about MIDI. This indicates that you are aware of the standard.

2. *between computers and musical instruments and synthesizers*   In multimedia environments, devices other than computers often come into play; your answer indicates that you are aware of this.

3. *sound boards*   In desktop environments, you often find yourself dealing with processors on devices other than your main CPU. You need to know this, and you indicate that you do.

References, and for further information

J. Ratcliff, "Multimedia Audio Systems," *Dr. Dobb's Multimedia Sourcebook*, Winter 1994, pp. 28–32.

Question 9   What do you know about Pentium?

Behind the scenes of the question

This is a straightforward question; perhaps the interviewer's company is considering moving to Pentium-based systems (or already has begun such an effort), and he or she simply wants to determine how much you know about the processor.

Suggested answer

"Pentium is *Intel's next-generation* chip, following the 486 (which followed the 386, which followed the 286, which followed...). Among its features are the use of *superscalar technology,* permitting two instructions to be executed per clock cycle instead of one. In general, Pentium *performance* is double that of the Intel 486 DX2 processor, with greatly improved *floating-point performance* for calculation-intensive applications. There is *a 64-bit bus,* and a *branch target buffer* which is used to try to predict which way an instruction will branch and increase the overall performance."

Key components of your answer

1. *Intel's next-generation*   You have some idea of the evolution of PC technology; you aren't a newcomer to the discipline.

2. *superscalar technology*   This is an up-and-coming microprocessor feature, and you are aware of it.

3. *performance...floating-point performance*   The name of the game with processors is performance, and you are up to date with the numbers and comparisons.

4. *64-bit bus...branch target buffer*   In addition to topics like clock speed and performance, today's processors are defined by facilities like those which you mentioned in your answer. Again, you are up to date with the latest processor technology, even though you yourself aren't a chip designer.

References, and for further information

"Intel Technology Briefing," advertising supplement, *PC Magazine,* Dec. 7, 1993, pp. 171–174.

Question 10   What do you know about PowerPC systems?

Behind the scenes of the question

As with the earlier question about Alpha-based PCs, and to some extent the question above about Pentium, the interviewer is probably trying to determine how well you keep up with the latest advances, some of which may be pertinent to that particular organization.

Suggested answer

"The PowerPC is a joint venture of IBM, Apple, and Motorola, and has been around since 1991. The first system just came out in late 1993. This is the *IBM RS/6000 Model 250*; it runs the *AIX* operating system (the only one available on this platform for now). *Apple* will introduce a *PowerPC* system pretty soon that will look more like a *Macintosh,* just as IBM's system looks like a typical RS/6000 workstation. In effect, the PowerPC is sort of like DEC's *Alpha* processor in that different operating environments from different vendors will run on top of systems based on the chip."

Key components of your answer

1. *IBM RS/6000 Model 250*   Not only are you familiar with the term "PowerPC," you also know of the system which uses it.

2. *AIX*   You are familiar with this operating system, even if you have yet to use it.

3. *Apple...PowerPC...Macintosh*   You are also familiar with Apple's plans for the PowerPC, and you recognize that one company's plans for the processor (e.g., Apple's) aren't necessarily identical to another's (e.g., IBM's).

4. *Alpha*   Even if the Alpha question wasn't raised during this interview, or if Alpha has no current role at that particular company, this lets the interviewer know that you keep up to date with many different aspects of desktop computing technology.

References, and for further information

J. Levitt, "A Close Look at the PowerPC and Some of Its (Likely) Brood," *Open Systems Today,* Nov. 8, 1993, p. 1.

Question 11   What do you know about CD-ROM for desktop applications?

Behind the scenes of the question

CD-ROM is "really cool stuff," right? The organization with which you're interviewing, though, is probably not very interested in using it for games, encyclopedias, or (my personal favorite) playing *Born to Run* or *The Best of the Doors* while you're working on your PC. The interviewer wants to determine how you would use CD-ROM technology for the organization's applications.

Suggested answer

"One of the best uses of CD-ROM systems is for storing *on-line documentation,* not only systems documentation but also things like *policies and procedures manuals.* There are a number of multimedia development toolkits available that can be used to help create multimedia documents that require *greater storage capacity* that is practical with today's PC hard disks."

Key components of your answer

1. *on-line documentation...policies and procedures manuals*   The straightforward component of your answer.

2. *greater storage capacity*   You understand *why* CD-ROM is growing in importance, in conjunction with the ever-increasing power on the desktop.

References, and for further information:

T. Hoffman, "Systems Development Simplified with CD-Rom," *Computerworld,* March 7, 1994, p. 40.

Question 12   What are the biggest trends that you see in printers that would affect how you would configure an office information system?

Behind the scenes of the question

Color printers, high-speed printers, dropping prices, alternative ink-jet technology...if your job includes developing office information systems, you *must* be familiar with as much as possible about printer technology—and pricing.

Suggested answer

"There's been a trend of late toward helping to boost *printing speed by using the Microsoft Windows Printing System* (WPS) to eliminate the translation step from Windows-based software into printer driver code. Another major trend is *directly connecting printers to LANs* instead of to servers. Technology like *600 dots per inch* versus 300 DPI is getting cheaper, along with color capabilities. You're looking at roughly *$1000* per unit for low-end systems (less than 8 pages per minute) and only about *$1500* per unit for those than can do up to 11 ppm. *Color lasers* are probably going to drop from around *$10,000* to half of that—*still more expensive than color ink-jet,* but certainly reasonable, especially if there are a lot of color printing requirements within this organization."

Key components of your answer.   In general, the above answer reflects knowledge of the following:

1. *base technology*   The references to 600 DPI, throughputs, direct network connections—you understand the directions in which printer technology is headed.

2. *pricing*   You are aware not only of current pricing, but also of pricing trends, including those of high-end products like color lasers.

3. *alternative technologies*   The references to color ink-jet printers show that for basic color printing, there are currently lower-cost technologies than color laser that may well meet the needs of many organizations.

References, and for further information

S. P. Klett, Jr., "Laser Printer Trends Go beyond Price," *Computerworld,* March 7, 1994, p. 37. Also see the inset boxes on the same page.

Question 13   What are the major types of laptop PC screens?

Behind the scenes of the question

This is a straightforward question—do you know the answer?

Suggested answer

"There are three basic types. The ones with the *lowest cost,* but the least clarity, use *passive matrix* technology. The *high-end systems* are known as *active matrix* screens. The typical passive matrix laptop runs in the low and mid *$1000's* now, depending on things like the processor and memory, while a fairly well equipped active matrix system runs *between $3500 and $4000.* In between the two of these, there are *double-scan passive matrix systems*; these are almost as clear as active matrix systems, but run about *$1000 cheaper.*"

Key components of your answer.   As with the previous question, your answer reflects two key things: the basic technology (you can always go further into the details of each of the technologies, but be careful not to elaborate too much if the interviewer doesn't seem really interested) and price. You are aware of both of these factors.

References, and for further information

Nearly every issue of *PC World, Byte, PC Magazine,* and numerous other PC magazines (including some dedicated exclusively to laptops) reviews laptop systems, discussing pricing and technology. Just pick up two or three of these periodicals and check out the latest pricing and product-specific items. Hint: Also scan the computer ads for pricing information.

Question 14   Do you think that fiber is a viable option for LAN environments?

Behind the scenes of the question

It's coming! It's almost here! The information superhighway! Everything in the world connected to everything else in the world by fiber—your office PC, your home PC, your television, your toaster....

Ok, enough sarcasm. The point is that this question, while not a trick question in the sense of an interviewer's deliberately trying to trip you up, is probably aimed at determining not only your network/LAN design skills but also your grasp of reality with respect to costs and technologies...much like some of the other questions we've explored in this chapter and in Chap. 9.

If this question had been asked around the 1991 timeframe, the answer would have been that fiber-optic environments were prohibitively expensive when compared with, say, unshielded twisted-pair (UTP) cable alternatives. By the early 1994 timeframe, though, the price gap had narrowed to the point where per-node fiber installation costs were "only" about 25 percent higher than UTP alternatives ($1500 to $2500 per system). In effect, you're currently (early 1994) looking at around $30 per node additional—which could, of course, add up in a hurry for the typical several-thousand-site LAN which might be considering fiber.

So, your answer should reflect (1) the price narrowing in recent times, and (2) the determination of whether short-term costs or long-term investments are driving a particular organization's spending decisions.

Suggested answer

"You're looking at around a *$30 per drop* additional cost for fiber optics versus *unshielded twisted pair,* which can add up over thousands of nodes, of course. It depends on what the *strategic directions* of the organization are, though. If you're primarily looking for *100-megabit-per-second data transfer,* and that will hold true for the next seven to ten years, then perhaps going with UTP would be a better, low-cost alternative, although there are *limitations to UTP* in terms of magnetic interference and the like. If, however, you're looking at something like *asynchronous transfer mode (ATM) for multimedia data transfer,* then maybe fiber would be a better investment instead of having to recable in three or four years."

Key components of your answer

1. *$30 per drop*   You indicate two key things in this answer: you know the price and you know the terminology ("per drop").

2. *unshielded twisted pair*   You are also aware of the logical alternative technology. You don't want to, say, compare fiber optics with thick-wire Ethernet cable for new installations; that's like comparing a 486DX2 66-MHz with a TRS-80—different generations of technology don't compare well against one another.

3. *strategic directions...asynchronous transfer mode (ATM) for multi-media data transfer*   Once again, you understand *why* technology is considered and are aware of technology trends such as ATM.

4. *100-megabit-per-second data transfer*   You know what the basic LAN capabilities are.

5. *limitations to UTP*   Along with the basic capabilities, you are also aware that there are limitations and potential problems with the lower-cost alternative that must be considered.

References, and for further information

S. P. Klett, Jr., "Fiber May Make More Cents," *Computerworld,* Feb. 21, 1994, pp. 49, 54.

11

Systems Software

As with hardware environments, systems software used to be relatively uncomplicated in the desktop arena, particularly on PCs. While multiple variants of UNIX (System V, BSD, SCO, OSF, etc.) complicated the workstation and server world, PCs were relatively simple to understand. IBM compatibles ran on DOS and possibly Windows, with a smaller presence for OS/2. In the Apple Macintosh environment, the generations of the operating system leading up to System 7 exclusively ran Mac systems.

Today, things are infinitely more complex, and you must be able to communicate to interviewers that you at least understand the overall systems software picture, even if you (like most others) haven't used each and every possible operating environment. By demonstrating that you have kept up to date with Windows NT, OS/2, Microsoft Windows, and other operating environments, you can convince your interviewers that you can easily adapt to any type of desktop environment.

Let's look at some of the questions you may find yourself being asked.

Question 1   What are some of the differences between Microsoft Windows and Macintosh System 7?

Behind the scenes of the question

To the layperson, there is little difference between the Macintosh graphical user interface (GUI) environment and that of Microsoft Windows, at least at the user's level. In reality, there are some subtle differences, and you should be able to convey your knowledge of these to the interviewer. Perhaps the company is in the process of selecting a platform for a new development project, and it is considering both Windows and System 7. Your knowledge about the tradeoffs may help tilt a job competition in your favor.

Suggested answer

"For the most part, the distinctions from a *user's perspective are relatively minor* today. Both the Macintosh operating system and Windows have *evolved* tremendously from earlier incarnations, in terms of utilities, *multitasking support,* and other features.

"DOS and Windows-based systems are more broadly used than Macintosh systems, with roughly 100 million DOS systems—20 million of them with Windows—and about 8.5 million Macintosh systems. This is mostly due to all of the IBM PC clones that came out in the early and mid-1980s, and the fact that users have stayed with those systems.

"The Macintosh is somewhat more friendly to novice users than Windows, with things like prompting the user to enter a disk if it's not currently in the drive, file naming conventions, and copying files and folders from one area to another. It also takes up less *disk space for the operating system*—5 megabytes versus 13 megabytes for DOS and Windows.

"A lot of the *horizontal applications*—word processing, spreadsheets, and graphics—are available for both systems and function more or less the same way...products like Microsoft Word and Microsoft Excel."

Key components of your answer

1. *user's perspective are relatively minor*   You have the foresight to put your answer in the context of a specific area, rather than make gross-level generalizations.

2. *evolved*   You know not only about today's technology, but some of the history; this give the impression that you have been involved with desktop computing for some number of years (perhaps longer than you actually have).

3. *multitasking support*   PCs are no longer single-tasking machines; you need to keep that in mind as you develop applications or build systems.

4. *disk space for the operating system*   This is just a tidbit, but it demonstrates that your knowledge is not merely superficial.

5. *horizontal applications*   The PC grew to prominence on the

strength of its horizontal applications (word processing, spread-sheets, databases, graphics, and later desktop publishing) and the tremendous advances in productivity given to its users. Recognition of this fact, and understanding that these functions still constitute the backbone of most PC usage in corporate America, will help convince interviewers that you are intimately familiar with PC technology.

References, and for further information

R. Sookdeo, "Mac vs. Windows," *Fortune,* Oct. 4, 1993, pp. 107–114.

Question 2   What do you know about OS/2?

Behind the scenes of the question

OS/2 has a role in some organization's desktop computing environments. Following a rocky start, the latest version, OS/2 Version 2.1, has been highly acclaimed. If you are interviewing for an OS/2 environment, you should understand how OS/2 fits with Windows and DOS environments.

Suggested answer

"OS/2 Version 2.1 is the latest release; in addition to "native" OS/2 applications, PCs equipped with this operating system can also *run DOS and Microsoft Windows applications.* You can run multiple DOS applications or Windows applications with *preemptive multitasking*; memory management is much more robust than that of DOS because of the 32-bit capabilities. Many *DOS applications run much faster under OS/2* than under native DOS. There are alternative configurations for running DOS and Windows under OS/2 that can be used."

(Hint: If you are interviewing for a position that involves heavy OS/2 usage, you would proceed to elaborate on the various subjects, answering technical questions as posed.)

Key components of your answer

1. *run DOS and Microsoft Windows applications*   You understand the relationship of OS/2, Windows, and DOS.
2. *preemptive multitasking*   You understand something about the architecture of the operating system and how applications and components can be integrated with one another.
3. *DOS applications run much faster under OS/2*   You have some

idea of the comparative relationship between operating systems' execution of the same applications.

References, and for further information

B. Bettini, J. Salemi, and D. Willmott, "OS/2 Performance: A Better DOS than DOS? A Better Windows than Windows?" *PC Magazine,* June 30, 1992, pp. 44–46.

Question 3   We rely heavily on our local area network environments; what do you know about network management?

Behind the scenes of the question

Putting a network together—achieving connectivity—is a relatively straightforward task in comparison to the process of managing that network. If you will be heavily involved with LANs in the position for which you're interviewing, you need to know not only about network operating systems but also about utilities usable to manage LAN environments (as well as other communications infrastructures with which your LAN connects).

Suggested answer

"You usually have to use utilities *above and beyond the NOS* itself to do the network management functions. There are *five different areas* that need to be managed: *inventory management,* in which the contents of clients and servers are tracked and made available to other users subject to permissions, *client PC monitoring, server monitoring, traffic monitoring,* and *reporting and notification.* One of the problems you find in PC-LAN environments today is the *lack of heterogeneous NOS support,* though this is being conquered though standards like *SNMP,* the Simple Network Management Protocol."

Key components of your answer

1. *above and beyond the NOS*   Just as the NOS is a layer above and beyond DOS and Windows with which you must be familiar, so too are utilities that aren't native to the NOS. You demonstrate that unlike mainframe and minicomputer operating systems with built-in utilities and management capabilities, *today's* PC environment is somewhat more fractured (through upcoming operating systems like Windows NT are likely to change that).

2. *five different areas...inventory management,...client PC monitoring, server monitoring, traffic monitoring,* and *reporting and notification* You demonstrate an understanding of the various disciplines of network management [and, of course, you would elaborate on whatever area(s) is/are most important to the interview at hand].

3. *lack of heterogeneous NOS support* You understand the limitations of some of the utilities, particularly in supporting heterogeneous multivendor environments.

4. *SNMP* Related to the above, you also understand standards-based solutions. Note that the OSI Reference Model–based solution (see Chap. 9)—the Common Management Interface Protocol, or CMIP—is far less mature than SNMP, so your mentioning of standards should avoid efforts that have little usage today (i.e., they aren't important in the context of the job).

Question 4   One of our biggest issues is applications integration, and we use OLE; do you know anything about that?

Behind the scenes of the question

In the spirit of cooperation among desktop systems and applications, standards have evolved through which applications can communicate with one another. Not to be confused with the Dynamic Data Exchange (DDE; see question 6), the Microsoft OLE (Object Linking and Embedding) standard, currently in version 2.0, is an emerging means by which Windows-based applications (and potentially others under the Macintosh System 7 O.S. and Windows NT) can be integrated with one another. Your answer should demonstrate your understanding of both the concepts and the current state of the technology.

Suggested answer

"OLE is a means by which compliant applications can be linked together in either a *synchronous or asynchronous* manner; the specification is *object-oriented* in nature. One of the advantages of OLE over *DDE,* which is another means of integrating Windows applications, is that the linkage can be done synchronously, with the calling application waiting in place until the embedding operation has been completed; with asynchronous embedding (which can still be done for simple linkages), there was no guarantee that the linkage had actually occurred in the timeframe expected.

"Right now, there are *some shortcomings* in areas like the lack of a common set of verbs and cross-network application execution; these capabilities should be available in future versions of the standard and with compliant product. Currently, *OLE servers are more common*; these are applications from which objects can be embedded in your own applications, in a client/server paradigm. Bidirectional interaction will become more common in the near future."

Key components of your answer

1. *synchronous or asynchronous* You are familiar with two different types of interaction paradigms among applications; they are suitable for different environments, and knowing how to use both is valuable (and not a skill that a lot of traditional PC programmers have).

2. *object-oriented* You understand object-oriented computing (and are prepared to elaborate if asked, to convince the interviewer as with our client/server and CASE questions in earlier chapters, that your knowledge extends far deeper than buzzwords and marketing concepts).

3. *DDE* You know not only about OLE, but also about DDE—you're just so gosh-darned knowledgeable!

4. *some shortcomings* As with other topics, you are aware of the limitations, so the interviewer can be convinced that you won't waste time spinning your wheels trying to achieve the impossible.

5. *OLE servers are more common* As with the above item, you know the scope of the capabilities available today, so you can convince the interviewer that you are indeed the right person. You could elaborate by citing OLE server products and their capabilities, if appropriate.

References, and for further information

"Moving towards Windows Building Blocks," *Byte,* December 1993, pp. 32–34.

Question 5   We plan to create a client/server database environment built on ODBC; what can you tell me about ODBC?

Behind the scenes of the question

PC databases (discussed further in the next chapter) have long been dominated by either stand-alone DBMS products (e.g., early versions of products in the dBASE family, such as dBASE II and dBASE III) or client/server products built on proprietary interfaces. As organizations put PCs more into the mainstream of corporate computing, there is a move toward client/server data management via standards-based *middleware*. One of the dominant standards is the Microsoft Open Database Connectivity (ODBC) applications programming interface (API). Knowledge of ODBC and compliant products will be a valuable asset when interviewing with many companies.

Suggested answer

"ODBC is a *middleware* standard from which an ODBC application *on Microsoft Windows* can interface with *multiple data sources*. The purpose is *to standardize client/server database access* rather than having to use a number of point-to-point interfaces in *heterogeneous environments*. The *driver manager* acts as an interface between the application and driver and the data sources."

(Hint: If ODBC is important to that organization, you would proceed to elaborate about compliant products, architectures, etc.; you should know the standard, product specs, and other documents *inside out* and have developed an application or two as part of your self-training program.)

Key components of your answer

1. *middleware*   Use of this buzzword represents "goodness" in that you understand one of the principles of constructing heterogeneous distributed applications. You should be prepared to elaborate on the term, since it's entirely possible that your interviewer will not be familiar with it.

2. *on Microsoft Windows*   Currently, ODBC is a Windows-only API; you demonstrate that you know this (though of course this may change in the future).

3. *multiple data sources*   You recognize the consolidation aspect of most corporate data environments today, given the reality of dispersed information systems.

4. *to standardize client/server database access...heterogeneous environments*   Related to your mention of "middleware," you emphasize that you understand the importance of standards-based development.

5. *driver manager*   This is an official ODBC term, and if your inter-

viewer is ODBC-knowledgeable, you demonstrate that you understand more than just superficial concepts.

References, and for further information

C. Hopson, "Developing with ODBC," *Data Based Advisor,* November 1993, pp. 88–101.

Question 6   What do you know about DDE?

Behind the scenes of the question

Like OLE, DDE is used for interapplication communication. It is an extension of the Microsoft Windows messaging system, and permits several types of interaction paradigms. Many organizations are developing Windows-based applications that need to communicate with one another, and DDE, like OLE, provides one way to do so.

Suggested answer

"DDE is a *messaging system* based on the Windows interprocess communications mechanism. There are *three different types of links* supported under DDE. *Cold links* require a client application to request an update from a server application, while *hot links* allow uninitiated updates to occur. Hot links can be turned off by using the *WM_DDE_UNADVISE* message, so that applications won't keep getting messages after they are no longer interested in receiving them. A *warm link* allows an application to be notified immediately upon data change but to hold off receiving the actual data until later."

(You would then proceed to elaborate on DDE protocols and other aspects as appropriate.)

Key components of your answer

1. *messaging system*   You understand the basic interaction paradigm, which is important.

2. *three different types of links (hot, cold, warm)*   You elaborate on your knowledge, emphasizing that different applications interaction requirements would use different models of communication.

3. *WM_DDE_UNADVISE*   Occasionally, throwing in a particular API call or syntax-specific item such as this one is desirable, lending credence to your experience with the subject at hand.

Question 7   Can you tell me about Windows NT?

Behind the scenes of the question

Windows NT has been heavily hyped in the past two years or so, and many organizations are wondering if they should incorporate it into their desktop environments. This operating system's multihardware capabilities (see the question about the DEC Alpha PCs in the previous chapter) makes it especially attractive. Because this is an extremely complex subject, it is recommended that you (1) read as much as possible about the operating system, its *initial* capabilities as well as those which will come down the road, and (2) try out the system on your own PC.

Suggested answer

Let's make this particular question a homework assignment for you. You might start by reading (several times) an in-depth article such as "Windows NT Up Close" (J. Udell, *Byte,* October 1992, pp. 167–178— this particular issue of *Byte,* while a year old at the time this is being written, also includes several other articles about operating system trends on the desktop, and is *highly recommended reading* as part of your training program). There are also many books about Windows NT that will give you even more information.

Question 8   What do you know about workflow systems for PC environments?

Behind the scenes of the question

One of the growing trends in the distributed desktop systems world is the incorporation of workflow technology into applications being designed and developed. Workflow, like groupware and other emerging models, is one of the areas in which someone trying to make the transition from mainframe or minicomputer technology into the desktop arena can establish a niche and become something other than "just another programmer/analyst."

The question itself is straightforward enough, but when asked by an interviewer, questions such as this one are intended to help establish that you have at least a cursory familiarity with the technology. A reply such as "I don't know what workflow is," while not necessarily a showstopper, may be taken to mean that you don't stay up to date with emerging trends and technologies.

Suggested answer

"You're starting to see a number of workflow tools for PC environments, ones like *Action Workflow Analyst* from Action Technologies. You can use tools like that to *automate the flow of different types of work* among system users, even when they're working on different PCs and other systems. You can also use the workflow map that is created and analyze the information flow, perhaps for the purposes of *reengineering* that flow to *make the organization work more efficiently.*"

Key components of your answer

1. *Action Workflow Analyst*   You not only know of the technology, you know products in that space.

2. *automate the flow of different types of work*   Better yet, you even know what the products do!

3. *reengineering*   It never hurts to throw in a hot buzzword now and then; just don't overdo it.

4. *make the organization work more efficiently*   It also doesn't hurt to emphasize that you understand that new technologies and models are most valuable if they actually contribute something to the organization.

References, and for further information

L. Radosevich, "Workflow Tool Strikes Human Chord," *Computerworld,* March 7, 1994, p. 49.
T. M. Koulopoulos, "Workflow Changes Its Image," *Computerworld,* Feb. 28, 1994, p. 97.
A. Simon, *Workflow, Groupware, and Messaging,* McGraw-Hill, New York, to be published Spring 1995.

Question 9   What are two different ways of sharing messages among systems within a LAN environment, and what are the tradeoffs?

Behind the scenes of the question

Everyone wants LANs, right? Install a LAN and all corporate and organizational problems will magically disappear.

If you are interviewing for a position that involves implementing LAN-based information systems, you will have to demonstrate that you know more than just "hook 'em all up and let 'em run" with respect to the computers and how they share information. This question is designed to ferret out that knowledge.

Suggested answer

"One way is to implement a system along client/server lines, with a split between client and server systems with regard to functionality within the environment. This means that the *servers must be available to run the applications,* since it's likely that the data will have to be sent to the client applications on an as-requested basis.

"Another way, which is simpler but *may not scale well as the LAN grows,* is to use file-sharing systems, with files of data sent across the LAN from one client application to another."

Key components of your answer

1. *servers must be available to run the applications*   You understand the negative implications of the first choice you discuss (or at least things which must be considered).

2. *may not scale well as the LAN grows*   You also understand that not only today's requirements but also tomorrow's must be taken into account.

References, and for further information

L. Radosevich, "Mail Users Face Quandary," *Computerworld,* March 7, 1994, p. 53.

Question 10   How might you implement DCE in a distributed desktop system environment?

Behind the scenes of the question

One of the hot areas in distributed computing is the Open Software Foundation's (OSF's) Distributed Computing Environment, or DCE. DCE is intended to be *the* open client/server architecture through which application components on heterogeneous platforms can communicate with one another. Chances are that if your desktop computing–related role in the position for which you're interviewing will go beyond basic small-scale LAN systems, there may be at least some peripheral work in the DCE space.

Suggested answer

"You could build a system in which PCs and workstations could access the *directory services* of DCE and request information about DCE servers that might be used for applications' specific needs. The clients would access server functions via *remote procedure calls* (RPCs)..."

(You could then proceed to elaborate on DCE facilities specific to that particular organization.)

Key components of your answer

1. *directory services*   One of the key components of any widely distributed environment, whether DCE-based or not, is the directory service. Components don't just magically connect with one another, and you understand this.

2. *remote procedure calls*   You are familiar with RPC models; you could elaborate on the DCE RPC models within your answer, if you feel it's appropriate.

References, and for further information

J. S. Bozman, "Wells Fargo Tags DCE for Bankwide Project," *Computerworld,* Feb. 21, 1994, p. 12.

12

Applications Software

Whether you will find yourself integrating off-the-shelf PC applications with one another as you create user systems or using applications like PC database managers (FoxPro, CA-Clipper, Paradox for Windows, etc.) to further develop users' systems, you need to have a great deal of familiarity with desktop applications software. In this chapter, we'll look at some representative questions of the type you are likely to be asked during an interview.

Note that as a computer professional (as contrasted with an end user), the questions asked of you will be more developmental in nature than simply being asked to recite product features of end-user software. For example, it's unlikely that you will be asked how you would create a three-column document in Microsoft Word 6.0; it *should* be assumed that if you were called upon to assist a user with such a function, you would either know it already or be able to use either the manual or on-line help to quickly find the answer.

Rather, you will find yourself asked questions of the type detailed below, those designed to help predict how productive you will be in desktop development environments. Not to overemphasize the point, but desktop development is often very different from that with which you are familiar, focusing not so much on programming languages as on platforms and even the developmental capabilities of spreadsheet managers. Your experience in these areas will help win a position for you.

Question 1   How would you develop client/server database applications using Paradox?

Behind the scenes of the question

Like most PC DBMS products, Paradox has its roots in single-user environments. It is desirable to move toward client/server usage, and organizations with Paradox may be interested in your knowledge or experience in this area.

Suggested answer

"You can use the *Borland SQL Link* interface to enable Paradox applications to act as front-ends for SQL server databases. There are a number of preparatory things you need to do, like *change Paradox field names* to remove spaces and special symbols so that they are more in line with those supported by the database servers. These name changes also have to be reflected in the *code and stored queries*. You then can use *SQLTools utilities* to move the tables from Paradox to the database server. Then, you create indexes that are needed by Paradox. There are other things that need to be done also, including changing application logic to *utilize the database server's transaction processing capabilities*."

Key components of your answer

1. *Borland SQL Link*   You are familiar with a mechanism by which a PC product may be integrated with server databases.

2. *change Paradox field names...code and stored queries*   Just achieving connectivity isn't sufficient; you need to do preparatory work to ensure that incompatibilities between products are accounted for.

3. *SQLTools utilities*   You know that tools and utilities are a quick way to perform many transition functions rather than tedious alternatives (e.g., unloading and reloading everything manually).

4. *utilize the database server's transaction processing capabilities*   You understand the limitations of traditional PC products in terms of high-performance areas like transaction processing, and you know how to reengineer applications to avoid "breakage."

References, and for further information

T. Colling, "Upsizing ObjectPAL Applications to Client/Server," *Data Based Advisor*, November 1993, pp. 163–166.

Question 2   For what types of applications would Lotus Notes be a good platform?

Behind the scenes of the question

Lotus Notes is one of the more highly touted desktop products in recent years, bringing groupware capabilities to environments that previously were built around standalone products and processes. There are limitations, however, to the types of applications for which Notes can greatly aid productivity, and as with programming languages, there are situations in which it makes sense to use Notes and others in which (at least in current versions) other development platforms might be more appropriate.

Suggested answer

"Notes seems to be *most appropriate* for document-based applications, but not necessarily transaction processing systems. Introducing Notes into an environment is somewhat different from introducing other applications because of *the impact of groupware on the workflow culture* within an organization."

Key components of your answer

1. *most appropriate*   As with programming languages, you can select the right platform for a given information systems application.

2. *impact of groupware on the workflow culture*   You are familiar with the two newest horizontal application paradigms, workflow and groupware, and the impact that they have on organizations.

References, and for further information

M. Faden, "Notes Champions: Job Isn't as Easy as 1-2-3," *Open Systems Today,* Nov. 15, 1993, p. 1.

Question 3   How would you use Microsoft Excel to develop end-user applications?

Behind the scenes of the question

To most PC users, spreadsheet programs such as Microsoft Excel are primarily end-user tools. These products can, however, be used as development platforms, and if you're interviewing in an environment that automates spreadsheet functions and manages user input, your understanding of how to do this will be important.

Suggested answer

"There are a number of Excel features that can be used to develop applications. The *command macro facility* allows programmed steps to be created and run by application users. You can create *custom dialog boxes that are dynamic,* that modify themselves according to user actions and selections. You can also create *custom help, commands, menus, and toolbars,* turning the spreadsheet platform into one specifically tailored to a given application. Applications developed this way should be approached the same way as other PC applications in that user requirements and interactions should be determined. You could use customized Excel in a *rapid prototyping* environment, creating applications quickly to get user feedback before fielding them across the organization."

Key components of your answer

1. *command macro facility*   Software development in the PC world involves more than just programming languages, and you are familiar with macro facilities of the type that are found in spreadsheet programs.

2. *custom dialog boxes that are dynamic*   You are familiar not only with dialog boxes from a user's perspective, but also with the fact that they can be customized and modified on the fly.

3. *custom help, commands, menus, and toolbars*   Along with dialog boxes, these are the building blocks of GUI applications; instead of lengthy, complicated programming language development for GUI applications, here is a rather quick alternative for those with built-in spreadsheet functions.

4. *rapid prototyping*   You understand the importance of rapid prototyping, and you see spreadsheet packages as one means by which this can be accomplished.

Question 4   What do you know about Microsoft Access?

Behind the scenes of the question

A relative newcomer to the PC database arena, Microsoft Access has gained favor among applications developers. This is probably a straightforward question (if a somewhat open-ended one) with the goal of seeing how much you know about the product and its capabilities.

Suggested answer

"Access is a *visual database environment,* through which you can *create drag-and-drop applications* and have multiple active tables, reports, and forms. There is a language called Access Basic which is similar to Visual Basic. You can use *ODBC* to get to *remote SQL servers,* so you can run Access in a *client / server environment.* You can also use Access to work with files and indexes of *dBASE, Paradox, and other PC products."*

Key components of your answer

1. *visual database environment*   You understand that PC database applications are far more powerful and robust than those of a decade ago (e.g., the early days of the dBASE family), and you can be counted on not to develop old-style applications in a "newfangled" environment.

2. *create drag-and-drop applications*   Same as above.

3. *ODBC...remote SQL servers...client / server environment*   PC database products typically don't operate in stand-alone environments in today's information systems.

4. *dBASE, Paradox, and other PC products*   There is more than one way to achieve interoperability, and you understand the benefits of mix-and-match products (e.g., using one product's facilities to get to data from another).

References, and for further information

J. Udell, "Microsoft's Windows Database," *Byte,* December 1992, pp. 51–52.

Question 5   What do you know about Xbase products?

Behind the scenes of the question

This is the type of question that in general has little to do with your qualifications for a specific job, but that nevertheless can provide you with an edge in a job competition. Consider a situation in which your interviewer has worked with many different Xbase products since the early 1980s. Your knowledge about the Xbase industry in general may be one of those small things that tips the situation in your favor by creating a kindred spirit between you and your interviewer.

Suggested answer

"When dBASE II was first introduced for CP/M systems in the early 1980s and later for MS-DOS, it became the most popular PC database product. dBASE III came out in 1984, and it dominated the market. dBASE III+ came out a couple of years later, and so did work-alike products like Clipper, which began as a compiler for dBASE programs. Soon there were a lot of products using variations of the dBASE language, including FoxPro. dBASE IV was introduced in the early 1990s, but by that time some of the other products had begun catching up in terms of market share. In 1992, all three vendors of the leading products using the dBASE language (which became known as Xbase) were acquired by large software vendors: Ashton-Tate by Borland, Fox Software by Microsoft, and Nantucket and Clipper by Computer Associates."

Key components of your answer.   In general, you shouldn't go overboard in your answer to the point where it detracts from the more important issues during your interview, but your indications of knowing about not only the technology but also some of the history and anecdotal issues may help enhance your credibility.

Question 6   One of the things we need to do for our Microsoft Access applications is build custom record locking for multiuser environments; how would you go about doing this?

Behind the scenes of the question

Unlike question 4, to which a general answer can be given, this question (and others like it) requires very specific details, indicating that your knowledge of the subject matter is sufficient for the job at hand.

Suggested answer

"Microsoft Access does have some *built-in locking, which can be modified.* There is a *LockEdits* property that can be set in Access Basic. Access doesn't lock an individual record, but rather a *2K block which also locks other records.* What you can do is implement an optimistic locking scheme at the Access layer and *build a facility* at the application layer that recognizes when a record is being edited and when it's been updated. At the application layer, you can write an entry to a shared lock tracking table while a record is being edited, and delete the entry after the update has been completed. You need to *keep track*

*of the table that receives the lock, the record ID, the user ID that origi-
nates the lock, and a timestamp."*

(You would then proceed to describe the other steps in the process,
including creating structures that SetRecordLock() and
RemoveRecordLock() functions can access, how forms are managed,
etc.)

Key components of your answer

1. *built-in locking, which can be modified*   It's often tempting to give
   an answer like "the product provides that capability," but your
   answer should indicate that in some cases the built-in capabilities
   aren't the most appropriate, and custom solutions are best.
2. *2K block which also locks other records*   You know the granularity
   at which the locking occurs and the ramifications.
3. *build a facility*   Again, custom solutions are often appropriate,
   and you know how to do this.
4. *keep track of the table that receives the lock, the record ID, the user
   ID that originates the lock, and a timestamp*   You know the things
   that must be recorded and managed to build the custom facility;
   better yet, you *already* know them.

References, and for further information

R. Maddison, "Building Custom Record Locking within Access," *Access Advisor,*
December/January 1994, pp. 24–29.

Question 7   We are installing an integrated application software environment, with word processing, spreadsheet management, database, and graphics; what do you know about these types of environments?

Behind the scenes of the question

Like the question about Xbase, this one has a historical flavor to it as
well as a technology overview aspect. The interviewer may be trying to
ascertain how familiar you are with *current* technology in this area
rather than older solutions that have been bypassed by today's products.

Suggested answer

"When integrated software first came out, there were packages that
had word processing, graphics, database, and spreadsheet capabilities

built in. These applications worked very well together, but were somewhat less functional than similar stand-alone applications. The stand-alone applications, though, were hard to integrate with one another, especially when they were from different vendors. Besides, different programs used different command sequences for similar functions.

"Today, you have packages like *Microsoft Office* in which stand-alone applications work together just as if they were part of an integrated package. You have *cut-and-paste* capabilities among the applications, as well as *live link* embedding by using capabilities like *OLE*. Command sequences on menus and toolbars are fairly standard among applications.

"One of the major advantages is that *end users can easily learn* to use these types of systems, even if they are relative newcomers to PCs. This helps provide rapid productivity among the user base."

Key components of your answer

1. *Microsoft Office*   You are familiar with this program group and its components.
2. *cut-and-paste...live link*   "Integrated" has several different planes, and you are knowledgeable about different integration paradigms.
3. *OLE*   You are familiar with OLE capabilities in PC environments.
4. *end users can easily learn*   The primary advantage of program integration is end-user productivity, and you are aware of this.

Question 8   We're looking at building a document management system; what do you know about this type of environment?

Behind the scenes of the question

Document management is a growing area for many firms. You can use questions that contain the phrase "what do you know about" to relate as much information as possible (trends, buzzwords, standards, etc.) in a relatively short answer.

Suggested answer

"There's a great deal going on in that area. I was just *reading a few weeks ago* about the Shamrock Document Management Coalition—that's the *multivendor initiative* working on *enterprise-wide* document management architectures and standards—and a new object-oriented API.

"You also have things like *SGML*,[1] which has a role in both *component document management* and *cross-vendor data exchange.*

"Another area is *distributed document management systems,* some using *text database* platforms and others using *relational infrastructures. I think* that the direction there will eventually move toward *object-oriented databases, possibly* ones based around *extended relational components.*"

Key components of your answer

1. *reading a few weeks ago*   You constantly keep up with *current* areas, not just those you may have learned about or worked with some time ago.

2. *multivendor initiative*   You recognize the importance of "open" multivendor solutions to most organizations.

3. *enterprise-wide*   Once again, the occasional buzzword never hurts...just don't overdo it.

4. *SGML*   A hint about the reference to SGML, or other acronyms: Sometimes it's appropriate to use the entire phrase for which an acronym stands; other times it's best to just stick with the initials. In this particular case, SGML isn't widely known outside of the document management and composition community. However, the full phrase, Standard Generalized Markup Language, is a mouthful, and in a way using it during the course of an interview sounds awkward, almost pompous ("look what I know"). Unlike, say, referring to DCE as the Distributed Computing Environment (a phrase which flows nicely), it's best to stick with the acronyms for awkward-sounding terms. If the interviewer isn't familiar with the term, he or she will probably ask you, and you can *then* expand on what the acronym stands for.

5. *component document management...cross-vendor data exchange* You are familiar with more than just the term "SGML"; you also know how the technology (in this case, language) is used.

6. *distributed document management systems*   You're aware of implementation architecture trends.

7. *text database...relational infrastructures*   This is related to point

---

[1]SGML is the Standard Generalized Markup Language.

6—you also have some understanding of different implementation alternatives within a technology area.

8. *I think*   This seemingly benign phrase can, when used strategically and sparingly, indicate to the interviewer that you aren't merely citing statistics and things you've read, but that you are also capable of formulating your own opinions about technology areas.

9. *object-oriented databases, possibly...extended relational components*   As in point 7, you have some idea about different implementation areas.

References, and for further information

E. Booker, "Group Seeks Open Document Access," *Computerworld*, Feb. 28, 1994, p. 1.

Question 9   How would you build access to a data warehouse environment for PC and workstation systems?

Behind the scenes of the question

It may come as a surprise to even seasoned mainframe and minicomputer database professionals, but a growing trend in information and data management is to implement *separate* informational data environments; these are commonly referred to as *data warehouses.* Your answer can indicate that you're aware not only of this trend, but of the underlying arguments and reasons for it.

Suggested answer

"One of the things you're seeing is a *new generation of EIS and DSS*[2] applications running on PC and workstation platforms instead of on the corporate mainframes. This means that the creation of a data warehouse environment is *probably* best suited to a client/server architecture, with a *data warehouse server,* which might even be *distributed,* doing the *data rollup* and acting as the *informational database server* for the EIS and DSS client applications.

"You could use some of the emerging database *middleware* standards, such as *ODBC,* to accomplish a great deal of this interoperability within an *open architecture.*"

---

[2]EIS = executive information systems; DSS = decision support systems.

Key components of your answer

1. *new generation of EIS and DSS*   Note that the question doesn't contain any references to EIS or DSS. This part of the answer tells the interviewer that you are aware not only of data warehouse trends and motivations but also of the related application models.

2. *probably*   Occasionally, use of words like "probably" is beneficial, showing that while you have a stong understanding of a technology area, you are not locked into specific implementation alternatives and are capable of accepting new ideas.

3. *data warehouse server...distributed*   You get more specific in the area of architectural implementations.

4. *data rollup...informational database server*   Same as point 3.

5. *middleware*   Once again, a timely use of a buzzword.

6. *ODBC*   Following up point 5, you know not only the buzzword but also standards related to it.

7. *open architecture*   A nice finale; it sounds good!

References, and for further information

C. Stedman, "Data Warehouse Access in Question," *Computerworld,* Feb. 28, 1994, p. 73.

Question 10   We're looking at building imaging systems using high-powered PCs; what do you know about these types of systems?

Behind the scenes of the question

Imaging is a growth area in the applications realm, and the interviewer wants to gauge what you know about this area. Like other "what do you know about" questions, you can use this as an opportunity to pack as much as possible into your answer.

Suggested answer

"There are a *number of technologies* that come into play with desktop imaging systems: *compression, OCR,*[3] *and also emerging areas like workflow, compound documents, and text retrieval. With today's high-*

---

[3]OCR = optical character recognition.

powered PCs, you have much better performance than in the recent past with respect to imaging applications.

"You can use technologies like *OLE*[4] for Windows-based object embedding and create desktop imaging systems *built around word processing and graphics applications, along with specialized software.*"

Key components of your answer

1. *number of technologies*   "Imaging" applications actually involve many underlying technologies, and you're aware of what they are.

2. *compression, OCR, and also emerging areas like workflow, compound documents, and text retrieval*   Related to point 1, here's a list to present to the interviewer to cement your understanding in his or her mind.

3. *today's high-powered PCs*   You know that PCs can play in imaging applications (as was noted in the interviewer's question), whereas a few years ago robust imaging applications probably required fairly high-powered workstations.

4. *OLE*   You are familiar with interoperability and integration technologies.

5. *built around word processing and graphics applications, along with specialized software*   As with most complex applications, a mix of "common" and specialized software is typically necessary.

References, and for further information

M. Vizard, "PCs Key to Growth of Imaging," *Computerworld,* Feb. 21, 1994, p. 39.

Question 11   Have you heard about HOST?

Behind the scenes of the question

Above and beyond basic I.S. technology, standards, applications, products, etc., many organizations are heavily concerned with industry-specific trends and support organizations. If, for example, you are interviewing for a position within the health-care industry, organizations such as the *Healthcare Open Systems and Trials (HOST)* are likely to be important to larger hospitals and companies.

---

[4]OLE = Object Linking and Embedding; see question 4, Chap. 11.

Suggested answer

"I was *reading about that in* Computerworld *a few weeks ago.* HOST's mission is to try to get a grip on the number of proprietary systems in the health-care industry, which is a *big problem with respect to sharing data among organizations.* They're looking at *testing laboratories* and *integration trials* where products and other new technologies can be tested before widespread deployment."

Key components of your answer

1. *reading about that in* Computerworld *a few weeks ago*   Again, you stay up to date with what's going on.

2. *big problem with respect to sharing data among organizations*   You are aware of major issues in an industry in which you're seeking employment.

3. *testing laboratories...integration trials*   With respect to this particular organization, you have some idea what its charter is.

References, and for further information

M. Betts, "Health Care Group to Test Open Systems," *Computerworld,* Feb. 21, 1994, p. 64.

13

Questions That *You* Should Ask

Even though there is a tendency to feel as if you are on trial during an interview, particularly if you are under the gun with respect to finding a job quickly for financial reasons, interviews should be viewed as a two-way discussion. You should, to the best of your abilities, try to determine whether the organization with which you are interviewing is indeed one for which you would like to work. Therefore, you should ask questions that will help you make your decision if you receive an offer.

Many of these questions are relatively standard, and apply to different types of computing environments or to the job market in general. Some, though, are especially pertinent to desktop computing (e.g., ensuring that you will be given the opportunity to maintain the currency of your skills and avoid future career disruptions like the one you are currently facing).

Question 1 How does the position for which I'm interviewing fit into the big picture in this company (or organization)?

What you want to learn

Are you being considered for a support position, a back-office job with low visibility? Or, perhaps, are you interviewing for a job that is in the spotlight at that organization, to be part of a team developing a major new system for internal use or for commercial sale? You should determine the status of this position, particularly from the points of view of job stability and job growth.

Factors to consider

If you're desperate for a job, it doesn't much matter. Otherwise, you should think long and hard about accepting a position that seems to have little potential for growth. If layoffs or other downsizing actions were to occur at that company, you might very well find yourself in a situation much the same as your current one.

What a crafty interviewer might tell you

Try this one: "This particular position will show us how well we can move you into areas of further responsibility."

An answer such as this one may very well mean that you are being considered for a position that does not have much visibility within the organization, particularly to those who control the dollar and promotion decisions. If the answer to your question is something like this, it is well worth pursuing it further to find out (1) exactly *when* you could expect to move into "areas of further responsibility" and (2) any other telltale signs of career turbulence not too far down the line.

Question 2   What is the company's philosophy regarding training and building new skills?

What you want to learn

Hopefully, the events leading up to your current job search have made you aware of the importance of staying up to date with new information systems technologies. While it certainly is possible to do so on your own time (as we discussed in Chap. 4), it's much more pleasant when the company for which you work has a commitment to ensuring that you and your coworkers receive as much training as is feasible. You could hypothesize that a company which makes a commitment to regular training in current and emerging technology for all of its employees is more likely to see you as an investment, a member of the team, rather than simply a body filling a slot for some short duration until the company decides it's time to dispose of you.

Factors to consider

Again, desperation and a race against the clock often tempers this particular issue. However, if you have some latitude and flexibility in your job search, you should seek out companies that are willing to train you not only in the products and languages currently in use, but those which may be important in the future (particularly to *your* career path).

What a crafty interviewer might tell you

"We believe in just-in-time training here." Translation: Don't expect any sort of training unless it is directly applicable to a task on which you are about to embark. Career broadening? Try XYZ Corporation on the second floor.

Question 3   What is the stability of this project for which I'm being considered?

What you want to learn

Given the vast numbers of wholesale layoffs occurring today, it is important to gauge the stability of the project for which you're interviewing. How solid is its funding? How important is the success of this project to the company's future? What has been the growth pattern (positive or negative) of staff members during the life of this project?

Certain industries are notorious for off-the-cuff mass dismissals (the defense industry comes immediately to mind). I've talked with numerous people who have taken jobs (frequently involving long-distance relocation), only to find themselves laid off a short time later.

Factors to consider

Desperation comes into play here, but unless you absolutely need a job immediately, you should look for a long-range commitment on the part of the company (or its customers) to the effort on which you'd be working. There are no guarantees, of course, and you should always have contingency plans in place.

What a crafty interviewer might tell you

"Our management has a strong commitment to see this project through to its conclusion."

It's unlikely that you'll hear anything other than a variation on the theme in the previous sentence. Would you honestly expect anyone to tell you that funding for a project is expected to run out in six months, and who knows if the dollars will ever be restored?

Consider, though, that your "reality timeframe" may vary if you are interviewing for a consulting position (see Chap. 14) rather than full-time employment. Even for a full-time consulting contract, a period of, say, 9 to 12 months might be considered to be long-term, while in the full-time employment world, a project expected to be of this duration would seldom be worth making a radical career change for unless the company makes a firm commitment to your postproject career there (and not too many do that these days!).

Question 4   In general, what is the company's philosophy with respect to career growth?

What you want to learn

This question is related to your question about the company's philosophy regarding training: You want to determine where you may find yourself three, five, perhaps ten years down the road if you join that organization. Will you be promoted into management if you succeed, and if so, will you still have the opportunity to remain hands-on with technology to avoid becoming obsolete and potentially disposable? Does the company have a technical track, through which you can be promoted without becoming involved in management (if that isn't your long-term objective)?

Factors to consider

The company's approach to career progression should be congruent with your own objectives, at least as you understand them at present. Otherwise, you may find yourself unhappy, as you eventually will find yourself doing something that you don't want to do.

What a crafty interviewer might tell you

"We are 100 percent behind career growth as soon as the project for which you're being hired is completed."

An answer like this is too generic, too noncommittal. Ask for an example, whether it is hypothetical for your case or, better yet, an example of someone who started there in an equivalent position and who now has progressed. What? No examples that the interviewer can think of? Hmmm....

Question 5   What is the company's policy regarding merit-based compensation?

What you want to learn

This is a laid-back way of asking the question, "How about profit-sharing? Bonuses? Raises that far exceed the cost of living? Stock options?"

Simply put, my philosophy is that people perform best when there is some degree of incentive pay (e.g., bonuses) for going above and beyond the call of duty; *good* companies and their managers recognize that.

Factors to consider

Perhaps financial compensation isn't your primary motivating factor; if this is the case, you have some leeway with respect to considering offers. If, however, your philosophy is "if I succeed and I make lots of money for the company, I want a cut," you should seek out a firm which shares that philosophy.

What a crafty interviewer might tell you

"We evaluate everyone down the road and, based on performance and accomplishments, will reward those who excel."

Like those to some of our earlier questions, this answer is far too noncommittal. Specifically, you should attempt to learn

- How the rewards are handled. (Raises? If so, how much? Bonuses? Again, how much on average? Promotions? Any or all of these?)

- What the evaluation parameters are to determine whether or not you "excel." What are the norms against which you are measured? Are they formally written, or arbitrary?

- And anything else that you can find out to help you determine what the reward-for-performance philosophy is.

Question 6   Is this a new position for which I'm being considered, or did someone hold this job before?

What you want to learn

If this is a brand-new position, you may view that as an indication that the company is growing and is on an upward trend. Otherwise, you should try to find out why the position is vacant. Perhaps the person who held it before has been promoted to new areas of responsibility, indicating that this position certainly has some growth potential within that company. If, however, four different people have held this position over the last year and all four have left the company, consider that to be a warning sign. This will be hard to determine, as it's unlikely that this information will be volunteered, at least before you join the company; you should try to determine it, however, by asking the question, "How long did that person hold the position before he or she left the company?"

Factors to consider

Again, desperation may temper your flexibility, but indications of walking into a potential hot spot should cause you to take notice and think twice about that particular company.

What a crafty interviewer might tell you

"The person who had this position before you, in fact the previous two people, just didn't work out."

Warning bells…"Excuse me, could you please expand on what you mean by 'didn't work out'?" You want to try to find out if "didn't work out" really means "ran screaming for the closest headhunter because things were just totally intolerable."

Question 7   Will my responsibilities include anything other than the position as it has been described to me?

What you want to learn

There are few things as disconcerting as accepting a job which you believe entails some number of functions, and then, when you begin work, suddenly finding out that you have additional duties, such as off-hours operations support. Or, worse, you arrive the first day and are told, "For the next two months, you won't be doing new systems development in FoxPro; you are assigned to a FORTRAN integration testing group. Have fun!"

Factors to consider

By asking this question, you get an answer up front as to what is expected of you in this job. If, after beginning work, you find your job has been switched or if you suddenly have a number of additional tasks of which you hadn't been informed, then you have legitimate grounds to complain to the management at that firm. This would also be an indication that your first impressions of the company may have been inaccurate, and you might want to reconsider your employment there.

What a crafty interviewer might tell you

"We often have new hires help out on special projects, but it usually doesn't affect your current work."

Likely translation: You'll be expected to do not only your full-time job but a whole bunch of other stuff as well. Can you say "after hours access key card"?

Question 8   Is there any travel involved with this job?

What you want to learn

Some folks like business travel (some *love* it), while others detest it. You should try to ensure that the travel parameters involved with this job, whether present or absent, match your particular desires, family needs, and other concerns.

Factors to consider

Of course, this should be tempered by other factors, such as how quickly you need to find a new position, but unlike other undesirable job parameters, such as embarking on a position with a relatively unstable history of prior personnel, walking into a job where airplane meals will become your diet staple if your family needs preclude travel can only make you miserable.

What a crafty interviewer might tell you

"There may be a bit, as the project needs dictate. We won't really know until Phase 2 of the project."

This reply may be on the up-and-up, or it may very well mean that "Phase 2" will take place entirely at some location in the middle of a desert somewhere, with an occasional weekend trip back to civilization. Try to learn as much as possible without appearing to be too negative about potential travel, if it doesn't matter too much to you.

Question 9   What are the schedule parameters for this job? How about work at home, flexible hours, etc.?

What you want to learn

You have to be *very* careful in asking this question, and you should pass on asking it unless you feel very comfortable that the interview has gone well. In general, though, for jobs which may involve long commutes, off-hours work, or similar attributes, it's nice to know that some degree of schedule relief in terms of working at home, working during hours when you don't have to fight rush-hour traffic, etc., is possible.

Factors to consider

You should try to gauge all attributes of a job. In addition to the obvious—whether you can beat rush-hour traffic, etc.—you can also tell a great deal about how a company feels about its employees. If it has rigid hours and just about goes by a timeclock, then employees may be little more than interchangeable assets. If, on the other hand, the company encourages productivity-enhancing working environments, including home offices and telecommuting, then this may very well be a company which values its employees and is likely to take good care of them.

Question 10   In addition to the regular work hours, is any off-hours support part of this job?

What you want to learn

More about the working environment. Working off-hours is one thing that should be explained to you up front. If "off-hours" = "after-hours"—that is, if you are expected to work regular business hours *and* do substantial after-hours support—then the company may be either short on cash or at best reticent on spending it, meaning that you will be expected to do, say, development, after-hours testing, and on-call customer support. In short, your life will shortly revolve around your job.

Factors to consider

Again, necessity and desperation factor heavily into how you use any information you learn in this area.

What a crafty interviewer might tell you

"There may occasionally be some weekend or evening support in addition to normal hours, as part of your training program."

A question: How long does "training" last?

Question 11   What constitutes successful performance in this job?

What you want to learn

For every position, there should be measures of the success (or lack thereof) of the person filling it. When it comes time for performance reviews and salary increases, it is to your benefit to be armed with as much information—facts—as possible regarding how you stacked up against the success criteria for that job. If, for example, you excelled at every one of the evaluation criteria, but an inferior raise is defended by a claim of "you just didn't do x, y, and z as well as we would have liked," it may very well be time to start looking once again.

Factors to consider

Again—not to sound like a broken record—your personal situation and degree of desperation should be factored in. If you desperately need a job *now,* then evaluation criteria a year from now don't mean much—but at least you may get some idea that your job search may very well resume not too far down the road.

What a crafty interviewer might tell you

"We evaluate each employee against the tasks that surface during the reporting period, and see how he or she rates."

Too general—there should be some well-defined measures that distinguish excellent performance from good performance from average performance from...

Question 12   How are evaluations done?

What you want to learn

This is related to the previous question; you want to learn whether this organization has a formal evaluation program, how frequently the evaluations are done, whether promotions are done in concert with annual or semiannual reviews, etc.

Factors to consider

Again, your personal situation should be your driving factor.

What a crafty interviewer might tell you

"We haven't really instituted an evaluation program yet, because we're a relatively new company. We're working on one now, and it should be in place in a few months."

With a new company, the above statement may very well be on the up-and-up, or it may mean that the company doesn't have the foggiest idea of how to reward employees for a job well done (and possibly not even the slightest intention of doing so).

Questions for Peer Interviews

In many interviewing situations, you will be interviewed not only by your prospective boss(es) but also by peers—those with whom you'll work on a more or less even footing, and possibly even those whom you might outrank. Peer interviews, though very often a pain (you often get shuttled from one technician to another, each of whom has little interest in interviewing you and has little idea of the types of questions to ask you), can give you an outstanding chance to get the real scoop on the company. Listed below are some representative questions to ask, given such a situation.

It should be noted, though, that interview sessions with peers shouldn't be considered to be informal "gab sessions." Remember that you're still talking to folks who will have input into whether or not you're extended an offer and, if you are, the level (and maybe salary) at which you enter the company. Retain all of your professionalism during these sessions!

Question 13   What training have you had in the past year? How does it rank with previous years? How about conferences?

What you want to learn

This is related to question 2; you can supplement the company's stated philosophy about training with hard data from those in positions identical or similar to yours. In addition to the actual information you learn, you can also be alerted to inconsistencies between the answers to this question given by management and peers. If, for example, you are told by a hiring manager or human resources interviewer that the company is firmly committed to professional career development, but you learn from a peer interview session that all training was put on hold three years earlier and hasn't been renewed, then warning bells should sound.

Question 14   How does this job rank with others that you've had in the past? What are its good and bad sides?

What you want to learn

Very simply, you want to hear a reply that is something like, "This is the greatest job I've ever had, the company is the best in the world." Folks in peer interview settings are often a bit more forthcoming about the downsides to jobs and companies; don't expect to hear wholesale badmouthing (companies usually don't put their most vocal malcontents into interview settings, or, if they do, they muzzle them), but body language signals—the roll of the eyes, heavy sighs, etc.—can give you cause to wonder about the job and/or the company.

In reality, you'll probably get answers like "there's good days and then there's bad days," and you can follow up these replies with *prudent* questioning. Don't probe so deeply as to indicate that you fixate on problems and deficiencies...use your judgment.

Question 15   What is the usual mode through which assignments are given? Do you have the information and tools to do your assigned job?

What you want to learn

There are two things you want to learn. First, you want to know how reasonable assignments are. Real life often demands last-minute gotta-have-yesterday situations, but if this is the normal mode of operation within this company, you need to assess whether you really want to spend your business hours constantly operating in crisis mode.

Additionally, you want to determine that once assignments are given, you have a reasonable chance of having the tools and information necessary to do the job. For that rush programming job, do you have a PC with adequate development software and capacity at your disposal? How complete are the requirements and specifications that you are given for development projects? Does someone blow a gasket if an unreasonable, nearly impossible assignment just isn't completed in the allotted time?

Question 16   How does management recognize a job well done?

What you want to learn

Just as with question 13, you want to compare management's and peers' responses to similar (but not identical) questions; this is the peer version of questions 11 and 12. People are often very candid if they feel that their efforts are unappreciated (and unrewarded), and even though they may not come right out and scream "they #$%@ don't!" the absence of a satisfactory answer (i.e., there is no mention of time off, company-paid team dinners, small cash rewards, etc.) may cause you to wonder about the company's willingness to reward employees for their success at achieving organizational goals.

In a roundabout way, you want to learn as much as possible about bonuses, raises, etc., without coming right out and asking about them (a politically incorrect course of action, in my opinion, especially if you're going up against truly desperate competitors for a position).

Question 17   What computing and development environments do you have? How often are upgrades done?

What you want to learn

A company that has a stated goal of providing all necessary tools, but that won't spring for a $1000 PC for a developer, forcing timesharing at odd hours, may not be the most desirable place for you. If the deadlines keep coming, but your hard disk is full and you can't get an upgrade, getting around the situation may very well add a great deal of overhead to your job functions.

Question 18   What is the camaraderie like here?

What you want to learn

You're probably not going to hear answers to this question like "I can't stand these people! What a bunch of losers!" Nevertheless, hearing about frequent after-hours get-togethers, the company softball team on which many of the employees play (and whose games most of the others attend), and the like gives you an idea that there is probably a somewhat harmonious atmosphere within the organization.

Question 19   Have you been able to work on the projects you've wanted to?

What you want to learn

Of course the needs of the company and the organization come first, but it's encouraging to hear that the managers make every attempt to allow people to work on projects and tasks that they really want to pursue. This gives you some idea that, for example, a two-month stint in the software testing organization won't become a permanent assignment.

Question 20   What is it like working with the customer?

What you want to learn

If a job is going to be a customer site situation, it's good to get an idea of the characteristics of that company as well as the one with which you're interviewing. Your new manager may be the most reasonable, easy-going person around, but if your job orders will be coming from a client manager who...well, let's just say lacks people skills, then the job situation may not be the most pleasant one. Once again (and for the last time in this chapter), you should factor your own situation into whether or not the answer to this question has any significance, but if you are choosing among multiple opportunities, an untenable client site situation may be worth passing on.

14

Interviewing for Consultants Only

Well, not *only* for consultants.

Recall that in Chap. 6 we discussed how consulting activities, even on an interim basis, can provide a bridge through which you can move your skill set into the world of desktop computing. Even if you are seeking contractual assignments rather than full-time employment, it is still incumbent on you to learn as much as possible about the organization and project(s) for which you are interviewing.

In this chapter, we'll look at 20 questions that you could (and should) ask during your interviewing process. These questions are designed to ferret out as much information as possible from your interviewers to help you decide whether to accept a consulting project if it's offered to you. Many of you may not have worked in consulting-oriented environments (or, more to the point, interviewed for such assignments) before, so these questions will give you some idea of the information you need to help assess a particular situation's potential and merits (or lack thereof).

Again, we should emphasize that your own personal situation often dictates how much weight you give to any red flags that arise from these (and other) questions. If you absolutely, positively need to find something quickly, then only a total showstopper (something along the lines of "we expect you to work for six months, and *then* we'll pay you!) is likely to cause you to turn down a project. Absent such desperation, you should *carefully* evaluate the answers you get to these questions, just as you would the answers to those in the previous chapter with respect to full-time employment.

Question 1   What are your payment policies?

What you want to learn

Consulting contracts are often handled differently from full-time employment with respect to how you are paid. You *may* be paid weekly, semiweekly, or monthly, in accordance with the number of hours worked on a project. Alternatively, you may be paid upon delivery of certain milestones (e.g., system subsets) or in some other manner.

Be *perfectly* clear up front, *before* starting a project, what the client's payment policies are. If you are using this particular consulting project as an "earn while you learn" opportunity—i.e., you are doing, say, Microsoft Access programming for the first time, and your client is "eating" your self-training time and learning curve as part of the overall project—be certain that milestone-oriented payments don't leave you with an uncomfortably long time between cash payments as you struggle with learning new software, hardware, and networking technologies...it may very well be a long time before you have a demonstrable milestone that would trigger a payment.

Question 2   Can you tell me about previous situations in which you hired a consultant?

What you want to learn

In a tactful manner, you want to learn as much as possible about this prospective client's past dealings with consultants or contract programmers. You want to be alert for

- Excessive criticism of past consultants ("we haven't had anyone in here *yet* who could complete an assignment on time!").

- Hints that the client is prone to adding new tasks outside the scope of contractual parameters. While such occurrences can be very welcome if you're working on an hourly basis, since they bring you new billing opportunities, if you're on a fixed-price contract, they can be, well, disastrous. Watch out for any indications on the client's part that he or she has tried to do this in the past.

- And general warning bells that indicate that a difficult working situation may be the norm with this client. Make sure that the scope of the project is realistic or, if not, that the "research orientation" is well established in the contractual parameters (i.e., your deliverables are based on report and study results rather than on functioning system components).

Question 3   What are the policies for accessing the user community?

What you want to learn

In medium- to large-sized organizations, your PC-oriented consulting may require some degree of involvement with the user community. From requirements collection to design validation to user interface testing to training, the success of your assignment may depend on steady access to the system users. In such cases, you need to ensure that you understand what the policies are for such access: permissions needed, accessible times, etc.

Additionally, you can try to establish the general mindset of the user community with respect to the project on which you're working. If, for example, you are responsible for a large-scale migration from a mainframe-based system to a distributed PC-LAN environment, the user community may be reticent about giving up character-cell or block terminals in favor of PC-based graphical user interface (GUI) systems—even though the system you're developing is "slicker," people are often resistant to change. You can try to assess such situations through the discussion with your interviewer about this topic.

Question 4   What are your plans for follow-on projects?

What you want to learn

The answer to this question will give you some idea of the steadiness of work with this client. You may be contracted for a six-month assignment to institute some Paradox-based applications, but indications from the client that "we have several consultants on staff who have been working here steadily for the past three years" and "we have big plans for this project over the next few years" may be comforting if you're looking for steady work. On the other hand, the absence of such indications probably means that you will have to start aggressively seeking new work near the end of this project (assuming you are hired for it).

Question 5   Has the hardware platform already been established?

What you want to learn

You should have some idea of whether or not the client has already selected a hardware environment for a particular project. This way, you won't go off on the wonders of, say, Alpha systems when the client has already selected PowerPC systems. If no firm decisions have been made, you can focus your discussion (and proposals and bids) on hardware analysis, if necessary, as part of your overall offering.

Question 6   Has the software environment—
the operating environment and
developmental software—been selected yet?

What you want to learn

As with the question above, you want to determine the specific environment that has been selected for a project or, if no determination has yet been made, if there are any strong candidates. You can then concentrate your study and preparation efforts on the chosen environment or, if none has been selected as of the time of the interview, you can use any knowledge you have about likely candidates to try to swing the interview in your favor.

For example, you might go into detail about the SCO Open Desktop environment as a likely candidate for workstations that the company is considering installing as part of its new office information system. Or, you could discuss the advantages of Microsoft Access as a development system if no database software for PC environments has been selected yet.

Question 7   What documentation would you
like to receive as part of this project?

What you want to learn

Many computer professionals who come from mainframe-oriented large systems environments are used to volume after volume of systems documentation. This is particularly true for government projects, such as those done in accordance with the U.S. Department of Defense's 2167A standard.

In desktop environments, however, similar quantities of required documentation are rarely the norm (though, of course, desktop-based systems done for the military would probably require voluminous documentation). As you prepare a consulting proposal and bid, you probably will have to factor in the time required to produce whatever documentation is either *essential* or *desirable* (or perhaps both, as in a subset of required documentation with options for supplemental volumes).

It's important to have a clear understanding of the prospective client's particular needs and/or desires to ensure that (1) your bid is prepared accurately in accordance with what you'll actually be doing, and (2) you can prepare your project schedules and proposed milestones accordingly.

Question 8   For custom software being developed, what level of exception handling, off-line "fixing utilities," table-driven software, etc., is desirable?

What you want to learn

In large, formal systems, it is the norm to have exception handling, data correction utilities, and other "noncore" functionality be as robust as possible. For PC-oriented environments, however, it is often difficult to convince a prospective client, especially a small business, that 200 hours' worth of excess development must be done in the areas described above. The client may, instead, be more inclined to call you in (or have someone inside the organization trained) to fix data errors, software blowups, and other such problems.

It is essential that you have an understanding of what the client is looking for in these areas before costing out software development tasks, to ensure that your proposals are in synchronization with the client's desires. It may be that the client would prefer bare-bones functionality initially, but after a few service calls to fix operator errors, you may receive additional work to install error-correction utilities. Similarly, hard-coded formulas that may make sense during the rapid creation of an initial system may be redone in a table-driven manner at a later date, after several years' worth of calling you in to modify program code to reflect formula changes.

Question 9   What past systems have been operational within this organization?

What you want to learn

If this organization isn't embarking on PC-based automation for the first time, you may be able to learn about potential trouble spots that you may encounter by asking this question, or one like it. Answers like "we tried to install a LAN-based system three years ago, but it was a dismal failure" should lead you to inquire further as to the problems. Some, like technological deficiencies in hardware and software, may be fixable today; others, like a lack of funding and/or high-level managerial support, may still exist, and could signify potential problems during your consulting work.

Question 10   How frequently would you like status meetings and/or status reports?

What you want to learn

This question has two components to it. On the surface, you need to have some idea of this particular client's feedback requirements. There may be a formal reporting mechanism in place at that organization that you will need to comply with. Alternatively, you may be left to your own devices as to how you will report the status of your efforts.

Additionally, though, by asking this question, you are implicitly telling the interviewer that you *know* that you are working for his or her organization, and that your efforts are geared exclusively toward getting its system up and running (or whatever your consulting task is). The interviewer will probably go away from the interviewing session with the impression that even though you aren't being considered for full-time employment with his or her organization, you have no doubt where your loyalties are supposed to lie during your consulting tenure. You may have secondary goals on your own part of building up résumé fodder in the desktop computing area, but the client's system is at the forefront of your concerns.

Question 11   What are the expense reimbursement policies?

What you want to learn

In many situations, in the course of your consulting or contractual activities, you will be incurring business expenses that are reimbursable. Such expenses may include the purchase of hardware or software, travel (including plane and hotel costs), on-line searches of product or literature databases, or nearly anything else *which is covered under your contract* (and you need to ensure that likely expenses and their reimbursement are covered in the contract).

You need to find out about the appropriate forms, average times until payment (you don't want to wait several months for the reimbursement of plane fare which you laid out yourself), whether the company will directly pay for expenses, etc. In short, make sure that everything you need to know is covered and specified in writing. If there is any doubt as to whether expenses (such as daily travel to the client site) are covered, make sure that those expenses are built into your fee structure.

Question 12   Do you have a particular contract, or would you like me to supply one?

What you want to learn

First and foremost, you want to ensure that there will be a written contract that defines at least the general bounds and scope of your work. Given that, however, you need to determine whether you will be required to sign a client's standard contract (in which case it is suggested that you consult an attorney, at least for a brief overview of the terms), or whether you can supply a contract which you have used in the past (or create specifically for this situation).

In effect, you are being polite by giving the prospective client the option of producing a contract rather than your simply thrusting one at him or her. Just as with the purchase of a car or a house, no one likes having a contract thrust at him or her with a "sign this now" attitude. This helps lend an impression of professionalism to you and your abilities, even if consulting is only an interim effort until you regain full-time employment.

Question 13   How closely will I be working with other staff members?

What you want to learn

Basically, you want to assess whether your efforts will be solo-oriented or group-oriented. Both types of situations have their benefits and drawbacks, and you should learn as much as possible about the working environment. Particularly if you are using this situation as an on-the-job training program in desktop computing technology, you should be sure that you will be given ample opportunity to explore in the course of your job without team members constantly looking over your shoulder, wondering what the heck you're doing.

Question 14   Who will I directly report to?

What you want to learn

On large projects in particular, you need to know where your direction will be coming from. Will it be from a project leader or group manager? Perhaps the user community will be directing your efforts, particularly if your work is focusing on user interfaces and reporting functionality. Be sure that you have a good feel for this in the particular environment, because you don't want to get in the position of doing what one person or group tells you, only to find out that the *real* coordinating authority wants things done differently.

Question 15   Is there any travel involved?

What you want to learn

Quite simply, you want to ensure that you understand the amount of travel (or lack thereof) involved in this particular project. There are consulting projects that take place almost exclusively at some distant location, with your on-site presence required. (In these situations, you need to fully understand the reimbursement policies, as noted in question 11).

There is a growing use of desktop computing technology in enterprise-wide computing, so don't assume that just because a particular project is PC-oriented, there will be no travel required. You may, for example, be asked to install PC-LAN systems at several remote sites, with some internal group tying those systems back into the centralized host via wide area network (WAN) facilities.

If your personal situation doesn't permit extensive travel (or travel at all), you need to be clear up front that there may be a mismatch with respect to this particular project and your likelihood of succeeding at it.

Question 16   Is telecommuting permissible in this job?

What you want to learn

First, you have to be very careful how you phrase this question, or whether you even ask it at all. In a "close call" situation, i.e., one in which you are on the edge of either getting a contractual project or not getting it, you don't want to pose any questions which would make it seem that you want to give anything less than 120 percent to the job.

However, with PC or other desktop technology, you may be able to do part of a project (maybe a little, maybe a lot) on your home system. Some organizations still have an "out of sight, out of mind" mentality, and don't favor telecommuting. Others, however, particularly in congested areas like southern and northern California or the Eastern Seaboard, would rather you not arrive at the client site every day already exhausted from fighting rush-hour traffic.

You may even find situations in which you can do long-distance contractual work for a company in another city or state with little or no travel to the client site; everything is handled via e-mail and modem transfers. Such environments are particularly suited for situations in which you need some flexibility of hours while you continue to seek full-time employment; you can work on client projects in the evenings on days when you are interviewing.

Question 17   [The level of dedication expected for this project]

Actually, this isn't a question, but something you want to try and gauge from your conversation that is related to the previous question concerning schedule flexibility (or lack thereof). You want to try to determine how much flexibility you will or won't have with respect to other needs, such as finding a full-time job.

What you want to learn

Phrases like "I expect instantaneous response and full-time dedication on the part of my consultants" will give you an indication that you may have little or no flexibility with respect to hours and personal situation items. Not that this is that bad, mind you, but it's worth noting that requests on your part for time off from the project may not exactly be met with resounding approval from whoever directs your work, and you will have to arrange interviews and other personal commitments during evening or weekend hours.

Question 18   What about off-hours support?

What you want to learn

If there is to be any after-hours support—if you are to be tied to a beeper and are expected to respond instantaneously to system problems—you need to know this up front. Additionally, your contractual arrangement should specify some time-payment premium in exchange for your constantly (or periodically) being on call.

Question 19   Would you like a complete package bid, including training, or just development?

What you want to learn

As with our earlier question about the amount and type of documentation, you want to gauge whether your competitive bid should simply include development tasks, or also include various types of training (systems and applications support, user, etc.).

Computer professionals who come from the ranks of large-scale systems development typically have little exposure to "what happens after we're done" other than maintenance. In most cases, a formal training organization will conduct courses for the user community or customer support staff.

In smaller-scale environments, though, the training staff is often synonymous with the development staff, and very often a single person—you—is responsible for all of both functions. You don't want to just drop off a system without adequate training (or documentation), but at the same time there are likely to be clients who would rather perform the user training themselves, something that is a bit easier in these days of graphical user interfaces than it was in the old command-line system days. Make sure you understand all of this up front.

Question 20   What are the most important things you're looking for from me?

What you want to learn

This is an open-ended question, but it is designed to let you know what the critical success factors are for this particular assignment. Even though your ultimate objective may be to use this project as a way station on your route back into full-time employment (but armed with new desktop computing skills), there are no guarantees that you will actually be able to do so...and you may be reliant on consulting for a much longer period than you had otherwise anticipated. Whether for future work or for references (and note that references are important as well for getting back into corporate life), you want to ascertain as clearly as possible what defines "success" in this particular organization and for this project. No one likes to do a project or job poorly, so it's best to understand how *not* to be perceived as having not done a good job on this particular project.

Index

Action Workflow Analyst, 156
Ada, 9, 35
Alpha, 59, 69, 131–132, 141–142
Apple Macintosh, 58–60, 126, 131, 134,
    138–139, 147–149, 151
Apple II, 68
Asynchronous transfer mode (ATM),
    145–146

Banyan Vines, 78
Business plan, 87–88
Business Week, 80
Byte, 80, 144

C, 9, 11, 24, 62–63, 73
C++, 24
Cairo, 126
Career paths, 22–26
CASE, 8–9, 23, 43, 52, 62, 113–115,
    122–123
CD-ROM, 142
Chicago, 125–127
Client/server computing, 57, 72–73,
    112–113
Clipper, 11, 34–35, 48–49, 61, 64
COBOL, 5, 7–9, 11, 14, 16, 23, 45, 62, 72,
    106, 112
Codd, E. F., 11–12, 61
CompuServe, 45, 65, 119
*Computer Professional's Survival Guide,
    The*, 22–23, 64
Computerworld, 42
Consulting, 75–89
    business plan, 87
    considerations regarding former compa-
        ny, 87–88

Consulting (*Cont.*):
    as an employment hedge, 75–77
    and interviewing, 187–196
    starting a practice, 78–86

Data Based Advisor, 65
Data warehouse, 168–169
Database skills, 61–62
dBASE product family (III, III+, IV), 11,
    13, 34–35, 45, 48–49, 57, 64–65, 77,
    99, 163–164
dbFast, 64
DB2, 7
DECNet, 14, 71
Development methodologies, 8–11
Digital Equipment Corporation, 5–6
Distributed Computing Environment
    (DCE), 157–158
Downsizing, 6
Dynamic Data Exchange (DDE), 151,
    154–155

Fiber optics, 144–145
Forbes, 80
FORTRAN, 5, 11, 14, 24
486 microprocessor, 5, 20, 59, 132–133
Fourth-generation language (4GL), 8,
    10–11, 62
FoxPro, 11, 43, 48, 55, 60–61, 64–65,
    76–77, 79, 110, 164

Graduating Into the '90s, 52
Graphical user interface (GUI), 5, 11,
    59–61, 73–74, 129–130
Groupware, 71

Harvard Graphics, 35
*How to Be a Successful Computer
    Consultant*, 3, 35, 44, 74, 78, 80–81

IBM, 50
IBM PC family, 14, 58, 68, 131
IBM RS/6000, 68, 141
IDMS, 55, 61
IMS, 55, 61
Informix, 7
Integration of products, 12–13, 70–71
Intel microprocessors, 58
Interviewing, 46–50
    basic guidelines, 46–50
    consulting-related, 187–196

Job searching, 41–46
JOVIAL, 13, 56

Local area network (LAN), 5, 59, 62,
    117–119, 156–157
Lotus Notes, 72, 161
Lotus 1-2-3, 35
LU6.2, 14

MacApp, 60
Majoring in the Rest of Your Life, 52
Microsoft Access, 55, 65, 76, 78–79,
    162–165, 190
Microsoft Excel, 35, 161–162
Microsoft Office, 166
Microsoft PowerPoint, 35
Microsoft Windows, 24, 58–60, 69, 72,
    134–135, 147–149, 153
Microsoft Windows NT, 69, 126, 131,
    134–135, 151, 155
MIPS, 68
Mobile computing, 69–70, 127–128
Motif, 73
MS-DOS, 149
Multimedia, 139–140

NetWare, 24, 62, 77
Network operating systems (NOS),
    150–151

NextStep, 69, 131

Object Linking and Embedding (OLE),
    151–152, 166
Object-oriented, 69, 113
Open Database Connectivity (ODBC),
    152–154, 163
Open Desktop, 190
Open Look, 73
Open Systems Interconnection (OSI)
    Reference Model, 124–125
Optical character recognition (OCR),
    169–170
Oracle, 7
OS/2, 147, 149–150

Paradox, 61, 63, 76, 103, 160, 163
Pascal, 9, 63
PC Magazine, 80, 144
PC World, 144
Pentium, 20, 69, 140–141
Personal Considerations (of job search),
    26–28
Personal finances, 92–93
PL/I, 5, 19, 62
PowerPC, 59, 69, 131, 141–142
Prodigy, 45

Quattro Pro, 78

Relocation, 91–92
Résumés, 31–41
    guidelines, 31–38
    sample, 39–41
Retraining, 55–65
    formal training, 63
    self-training, 57–63

SCSI, 136–137
Self-assessment, 18–28
SNA, 5, 14
SQL, 11–12, 43, 124–125
SQLBase, 33
Standard Generalized Markup Language
    (SGML), 167

Sun MicroSystems, 68
Systems migration and transition, 71

Taligent, 69
Technical skills, 19–20
Third-generation language (3GL), 9, 13
TRS-80, 68, 145
TurboC, 9
TurboPascal, 10

Unisys Corporation, 13
UNIX, 5, 59, 68–69, 132, 134, 147

VAX minicomputer, 5–6, 71, 112
VAXnotes, 71
Visual Basic, 63, 163

What Color Is Your Parachute?, 28, 153
Wide area network (WAN), 5
Workflow, 72, 155–156
Writing a Job-Winning Resume, 53

Xbase, 11, 35, 43, 65, 163–164
XWindows, 60

ABOUT THE AUTHOR

Alan Simon is the author of four computing books published by McGraw-Hill, including the best-selling *How to Be a Successful Computer Consultant* (praised as "required reading" by *Computing Reviews* and now in its Third Edition), *The Computer Professional's Survival Guide*, and *The Computer Professional's Guide to Effective Communications*. He has held many staff and consulting positions in the computer industry since 1979. Mr. Simon lives and works in Jackson, New Jersey.